# TEENS CAN BOUNCE BACK

# TEENS *Can* BOUNCE
# BACK

**:rails**

## HORIZON BOOKS
### CAMP HILL, PENNSYLVANIA

# HORIZON BOOKS

A Division of Christian Publications, Inc.
3825 Hartzdale Drive, Camp Hill, PA 17011
www.cpi-horizon.com
www.christianpublications.com

*Teens Can Bounce Back*
ISBN: 0-88965-180-9
© 2000 by Diana L. James
LOC Catalog Card Number: 99-080156

Lovingly dedicated to my truly terrific
teen (and near teen) grandkids:
Ricky, Alan and Lorinda.
I believe in you!

# Contents

## Section 2  Straight from the Teens

## Section 3  My Own Special Teenage Kid

## Section 4  What I Learned from Working with Teens

# Section 5  Advice from the Experts

## Acknowledgments

A thousand thanks to my husband, Max, without whose amazing talents, dedicated help and ever-ready encouragement this book might never have been completed.

Heartfelt thanks to the wonderful people of all ages who cared enough about teens to contribute their personal stories of victory and hope.

*Introduction*

This book is for teens and those who care about them. It is a collection of true stories and observations told with affectionate understanding of the struggles and pressures faced by young people in today's society. It is also designed to give an emotional and spiritual boost to teens, any teens, but perhaps especially those who may be at a low point or who may be facing important life decisions.

Some of the stories are written by teens themselves, giving expression to their hopes and fears, their uncertainties and their deepest beliefs. Some are written by parents who have fretted and fumed, laughed and cried through the ups and downs of raising a teenager.

Several popular and well-known youth leaders and youth pastors, plus musicians whose music is popular with Christian youth, have contributed stories telling some of the lessons they have learned over their years of working "in the trenches" with teenage kids. These outstanding people have contributed stories written in their own unique, sometimes "off the wall" styles, giving the book a dash of humor and a splash of pizzazz.

Other stories here included are told by men and women who lived through some really terrible or frightening experiences when they were in their teens. But each turned to God through Scripture and prayer, either alone or through the ministry of believing friends and found a lifeline in their time of need.

I have been deeply disturbed by recent statistics and news reports indicating an alarming increase in the frustration, anger and confusion being felt by many teenagers today. Although the teen years have always been known as a period of turmoil because of rapid physical and emotional changes during that time, now life seems a hundred times more difficult because of the increasingly negative and immoral influences that bombard all of us from every direction.

I put this book together because I want to present a brighter, more encouraging picture. I want teens and those who care about them to read the true experiences of people (many of whom are well-known to them) who have gone through rough times too but have emerged from their struggles wiser, stronger, spiritually deeper and personally more compassionate toward the sufferings of others.

I pray that these stories will encourage you, inspire you and give you hope. As you read each one, the message comes through loud and clear: "No matter how tough things get—teens *can* bounce back!"

—DLJ

## Section 1

## When I Was a Teen

*Remember not the sins of my youth
and my rebellious ways;
according to your love remember me,
for you are good, O LORD.*
                                    (Psalm 25:7)

Most adults can look back and remember experiences from their teen years that stand out as lessons learned the hard way. Sometimes there was a sudden flash of spiritual awareness or a mental "Ah-ha!" Other times the learning was a slow growth process, and the lessons became clear only later as they looked back at their mistakes through the other end of the telescope of time.

The stories in this section bring wisdom gained in either or both of these two ways. The writers are no longer in their teens, but some remember clearly how painful, confusing and sometimes lonely the teen years were for them. Others revisit their teen experiences with humor.

Whether heavy or light, all give hope and encouragement for today's teenager. The underlying message: "If *I* could make it through the dangerous minefield of those teen years, so can you."

## Michael W. Smith

hen I was in high school I played piano, but I lived for baseball. I envisioned myself someday in front of cheering crowds holding a bat, not a microphone. Then, when I was fifteen, I didn't make the all-star team. My dream was suddenly crushed. I had no idea that the closing of that door would open another that was far beyond what I could have possibly imagined.

I had become a Christian when I was ten and was active in our family's church, but my involvement increased when my baseball career ended. Every Sunday night I played piano for our praise gatherings. Our youth choir performed incredible musicals, which featured music that was very different from the hymns we sang on Sunday morning. I started listening to artists from the Jesus movement of the early

5

'70's, and I liked what I heard. I "delighted" in the music and the friendships that I found in my youth group. Only looking back years later do I see that God was planting the seeds of desire so that I would grow into my career in music.

Just as Christ told a parable about young plants choked out by weeds, my story could have had a similar ending. As you're about to discover, my journey involved a detour that could have destroyed all that I now cherish. Perhaps you can learn from my mistakes.

After growing up in a loving Christian home, giving my heart to Christ as a boy and being involved in a great church, I hit the skids my junior year of high school. Some of my closest friends graduated and moved off to college or got married. Without that circle of support, I started hanging out with people who offered me everything I had managed to avoid up to that point. I was testing limits, taking chances and acting crazy.

When I moved to Nashville in 1978, I sank deeper into that lifestyle. Because I was no longer under the protective eyes of my small-town family and friends, I responded to my newfound freedom with more habits that enslaved me. I kept late hours and wouldn't wake up until afternoon. I was experimenting with drugs and trying to impress people with how cool I was. Instead of acknowledging my musical abilities as a precious gift from God, I took them for granted.

With each step deeper into the mire, I grew more unhappy, more depressed. One night after the band I was in had played at a bar, everybody in the band went over to one guy's house to party. There I made a near fatal error by trying a drug that caused an extremely violent reaction. On the way home I thought I was losing my mind. I stayed up all night, terrified about what had happened. I remember praying over and over, "God, don't let me die." The next day I began to recover from the ordeal, but I still didn't take the very large hint to run from that lifestyle.

During a visit to my parents' home, I vividly remember having a quiet but uncomfortable conversation with my father on the porch. With knowing eyes, he softly said, "You're going to have to straighten out your life." He knew that I didn't need a lecture. His few words communicated both the hurt and the love that he felt. Even though I knew my dad was right, I didn't have the faith and self-control to turn from the dead-end alley I was traveling.

In October 1979 I had an experience that I would describe as similar to a minor nervous breakdown. Psalm 38 paints a pretty accurate picture of what was going on inside me:

> For my iniquities have gone over my
>   head;
> Like a heavy burden they are too heavy
>   for me.

*My wounds are foul and festering
Because of my foolishness.
I am troubled, I am bowed down greatly; I go
mourning all the day long. (38:4-6, NKJV)*

The day I hit bottom I was alone in the house. I began to freak out. My thoughts raced. My heart pounded. My body shook. For hours, I lay on the kitchen floor, curled up like a baby.

I can't explain all that was going on inside me, but there came a specific moment when I felt that God joined me there on the floor. He didn't come to condemn me or reprimand me. I already knew that my life was totally out of control. Instead, He came to lift the burden that was crushing me and to free me to start again. Inside I knew that God was saying, *This is your turning point.* The next day I could sense my life was taking a new direction.

Although things have not been all blue skies and rainbows since those reckless years, I've come to recognize that God's ways are far better than mine. Just as my life turned from self-destruction, God started to give me glimpses of what lay in store if I would just delight myself in Him:

*For I know the thoughts that I think toward you, says the LORD, thoughts of peace and not of evil, to give you a future and a hope. Then you will call upon Me and go and pray to Me, and I will listen to you. And you will seek Me and find Me, when you search for Me with all your heart. I will be found by you, says the*

*LORD, and I will bring you back from your*
*captivity. (Jeremiah 29:11-14, NKJV)*

The Lord really did bring me back from being
captive—from being cool and acting in total rebellion—to doing what I knew to be right.

Don't deceive yourself by thinking you are too
strong or smart to stumble. At fifteen, I would
have said there was no way I would ever place
myself in some of the situations that grew far too
familiar. Sin will take you farther, keep you longer and cost you more than you can ever see at
the outset.

Right now, are you a prisoner to anything? Resist the temptation to quickly answer "No!" and
read on, because I don't want you to speed beyond something so important.

Are you trapped by your image, your ego or
your pride? Have you been covering up an addiction to pornography, clothes or food? Do you
have a clean slate before God with sexuality?
Are there people you refuse to forgive? Is it easy
to excuse jealousy or rage?

If you are being held captive, Christ offers the
key to your freedom. He said, "Whoever com-
mits sin is a slave of sin. And a slave does not
abide in the house forever, but a son abides forever. Therefore if the Son makes you free, you
shall be free indeed" (John 8:34-36, NKJV).

Start by confessing that sin to God. Then if
you have wronged other people, do everything
in your power to make it right. If you need to

have someone pray for you to help you get rid of the guilt and shame, find someone trustworthy and come clean.

Not only will the Son make you free, but His Father has promised to give you a future and a hope.

In my travels, I've met people who feel stuck, believing that their lives will never change for the better. They think that today is the same as yesterday and tomorrow will be no better. To borrow a song title from Steven Curtis Chapman, there really is "more to this life."

Whether you're in high school or college, you're preparing to write the next chapter of your life. Can you sense if seeds have been planted in you? How ready do you feel? What's going to give structure to what lies ahead?

With all my heart, I believe that God's Word will give more insight on who you are and how to live than any class or seminar you will attend, any training program you will complete or any textbook you will read. I know a man whose Bible has the words "Manufacturer's Handbook" tooled into its leather cover. You may think that's a little corny, but it's true. Who could possibly know more about life than the One who created it?

*Photo courtesy of Reunion Records.*

Michael W. Smith is one of contemporary Christian music's most popular artists. He is the composer of such contemporary classics as "Great Is the Lord" and "Thy Word." He has won an American Music Award, two Grammy Awards and seven Dove Awards. As the best-selling male artist in Christian music, Michael W. Smith has had a string of hits that have topped both Christian and pop radio charts. Michael's keyboard artistry has been recognized by appearances with symphony orchestras, sold-out concert tours, requested performances by presidents, the Pope and fans throughout the world.

## Fear Not!

### Nancy Moser

*Fear of man will prove to be a snare,*
*but whoever trusts in the LORD is*
*kept safe.*

(Proverbs 29:25 )

'm afraid of fear. It's an emotion I'd rather not visit. And it's an emotion I definitely don't want my kids to visit. And yet fear and childhood are deeply entangled, like gnarled trees whose barren branches grab at lightning flashes in the sky while the rumble of thunder makes the earth shake. . . .

Enough! We have an amazing power to get ourselves worked up over nothing. As a teenager I very foolishly watched the Saturday night *Creature Feature* (hosted by Dr. Sanguinary) alone in the basement. I'd wrap myself in a blanket and snuggle into the deep recesses of the Naugahyde chair so only my eyes would show. The lights were off (mood lighting for monsters) and the flickering of the movie cast strange shadows behind the sewing machine and the Ping-Pong™ table. No matter how scared I got, it never occurred to me to shut off the TV. Maybe it was because I knew all monsters (at least in movies shown in the '60s) got their what-for in the end. Mankind prevailed and was victorious.

In the movie's aftermath, there was the problem of getting from the basement to my bedroom upstairs without the TV monsters grabbing me by the tail. As the credits rolled and I ventured from my cocoon to turn *on* the light and *off* the TV—in that order—I kept the blanket wrapped around me. Everyone knows that monsters cannot penetrate Orlon® and wool (cotton is questionable). Without the noise of the TV, the silence of the house was deafening. But if I listened carefully, I could hear *them*. I could hear the monsters in the furnace room slithering around my dad's tools, their claws scratching on the floor as they made their way to the rec room to get. . . .

I ran up the stairs. I tripped on the blanket. I could *feel* the monsters nipping at my heels, and my spine tingled with their presence. I stumbled into the bedroom hallway only to stop dead in my tracks as I spotted a dark form. . . .

"What's going on?" my mother asked, flipping on the hall light.

I gathered as much dignity as I could muster with flushed cheeks, wild eyes and a blanket tangled around my legs. "Uh, uh . . ."

"You scared yourself watching those monster movies again, didn't you?"

To prove her wrong I let the blanket pool at my feet, risking the cold rush of monster vibrations on my shoulders. I straightened my spincless spine and strode into my room. "I'm going to bed now," I proclaimed.

My mother smiled a knowing smile. "Do you want me to check your closet for bogeymen?" she asked.

"That won't be necessary." *I'll check the closet myself.*

I knew there were no bogeymen, no Frankensteins, no wolf-men, no gelatinous blobs from outer space. Yet once in a while, I invited them into my life. Why? Was it so I could conquer them? Was I that desperate for a thrill or a victory?

As I grew older I discovered there were plenty of real things to be afraid of. Such as going away to college, getting married—or not getting married. Bills, kids, failure, wrinkles . . .

I didn't need to invite fear into my life. It was all around me. Sometimes I'd find myself being worried about being worried. What if the worst happened? What would I do if . . . I gave fear a lot of power it didn't deserve.

My niece Brittney started kindergarten this year. As Halloween approached, the school counselor talked to the kids about fear, mentioning that she used to have a ritual before bedtime where she would check under her bed and in her closet for any monsters. Brittney raised her hand and said, "My dad won't allow monsters in *our* house."

It's so simple. We'll never have to worry about being afraid, about checking our lives for the bogeymen and monsters—if we don't allow them into our house. And how do we do that?

By snatching the power away from fear and giving it to God. Now that's a thrill. That's a victory.

From *Save Me, I Fell in the Carpool,* by Nancy Moser, © 1997 by Nancy Moser. All rights reserved. Servant Publications, Ann Arbor, Michigan. Used by permission.

Since "overcoming fear with the power of God's love," as Nancy Moser puts it, she has had five books published and has become an inspirational speaker. The first two books in her Christian fiction series are out: *The Invitation* and *The Quest.* "Fear Not" is taken from her book of inspirational humor, *Save Me, I Fell in the Carpool.* Other humor books by Nancy Moser include *Motherhood: A Celebration of Blessings & Blunders,* and *Expecting: Celebrating the Waiting & the Wonder.*

Address: 11326 W. 141st St., Overland Park, KS 66221
E-mail: Bookmoser@aol.com

# My Foolishness, His Faithfulness

## Scott Krippayne

*I will sing of the LORD's great love*
*forever;*
*with my mouth I will make your*
*faithfulness known through all*
*generations.*

(Psalm 89:1)

I feel a lot like the psalmist. I want to talk about, sing about and share God's faithfulness. I've experienced it firsthand.

One year after I accepted Jesus as my Lord and Savior, it was time to head off to college. I grew up in a rather small town in a somewhat protective family, and I was a bit naive about the big city and a big college. My new experiences were eye-opening to say the least. I felt lost among 35,000 other students. I was Student

Number 8832091—I felt more known by my number than my name.

During my first quarter there, I could go to classes for a week and not see anyone I knew. I was lonely and wanted desperately to fit in. Having those feelings and living away from my parents for the first time made me quite susceptible to peer pressure. And it didn't take that much pressure for me to cave in: "Do you want a beer?" was usually enough to do it. Without going into all the details, my Bible went on the shelf, and I went to the parties.

I made a lot of bad choices my freshman year, but the Lord refused to let me go. I wanted to put our relationship on hold, but He wasn't willing to let that happen. God pursued me and He was persistent. And I'm glad He was. I knew the choices I was making weren't the best and that God had something better, but I continued to disobey. I knew my lifestyle wasn't His will, but I was selfish. I'd look at my Bible, think of my relationship with the Lord, and find it hard to face Him—a holy God.

But through it all, He never gave up on me. He used different people in my life to remind me of the truth. He would bring people into my room, and they would ask about my Bible. I started getting invited to a college fellowship that met near campus. It soon became evident that I would have to address my relationship with the Lord. I would have to face God. Eventually, I began going to that college fellowship. I started reading my Bible again, I confessed my sins and I began to make better choices.

I was foolish, but the Lord was faithful. I may have let Him down, but He wasn't going to let me go. When I ran away, He guided me back home. I broke my promise to live for Him, but He kept His promise—He didn't leave. He loved me through my struggles.

Sometimes I look back and wish I could live that year over and make some different choices—not be so foolish. But I learned a great deal about the character of God during that time. I learned that He loves us enough to pursue a relationship with us. And I learned that He is persistent in His pursuit. No one is a lost cause. We have a God who is faithful and a God who forgives.

Think of some examples of God's faithfulness in your own life. Has He brought you through some difficult times? Are you in the midst of a hardship now? Do you see the Lord's hand in your life? Keep watching. Our Lord will prove Himself faithful. He has proven Himself so time and time again.

As I see the Lord demonstrate His character—His love and His faithfulness in our lives—I'm amazed. And I'm grateful. And I want to leave my foolishness behind and become like the psalmist and "sing of the LORD's great love forever" and make His "faithfulness known through all generations." Let's go out and make it known.

*Photo courtesy of Mike Atkins Management*

Scott Krippayne has had over twenty-five of his songs recorded by over fifteen artists with many chart toppers including "Jesus Doesn't Care," recorded by Point of Grace. In 1997, Krippayne received a Dove Award nomination for Inspirational Song of the Year for his number one song, "Sometimes He Calms the Storm." He was recently named Top Christian Artist of the Year by *American Songwriter* magazine.

# Who Is That Woman?

## Marie Asner

As a teenager, I had a wretched case of acne. Every night I would pray, "Please God, change me. I don't like the way I look." In the morning, there would be the same me in the mirror. I tried to hide my appearance with different eyeglasses, makeup and hairstyles.

Sometimes, kids would tease me and call me "red face." One doctor thought makeup was causing the acne problem and advised me to "go plain." Another had me wash my face in buttermilk, but still the acne remained.

I was unhappy with my hair color too. Being a brunette in a town of mostly brunettes was definitely not a plus. The advertising phrase, "Blondes Have More Fun," was current and I decided this was for me. My mother wouldn't hear of a hair-color change, so in secret I bought a blonde wig from a wig catalog to cover my brunette hair. I figured God really wanted me to be a blonde, but

21

somehow it didn't happen. So I decided to help a bit. I raced my family to the mailbox every day for weeks until the package arrived. "Contents: Wig" would have been a giveaway.

I tried it on every evening after everyone was asleep and thought I looked fine—but where to wear it and bring out the "new me"?

During summer vacation I was going to visit a cousin in another state. Traveling by bus was the economical and "common folks" way to go, but I decided to make this a "glamorous" trip. When my mother took me to the bus depot I begged her not to wait until the bus left, but just to drop me off and I would be fine. She reluctantly agreed.

As soon as she drove away, I dashed into the ladies' room and impatiently waited until everyone left so I could begin the transformation. I donned heavy makeup to cover the acne and put on the blonde wig, carefully tucking my dark hair beneath. My, was I ever something else!

Then, as poised as possible, I left the ladies' room and stood in line for the bus, happily oblivious to any stares around me.

The journey began and I found the wig clinging to the back of the seat. I had to sit upright in order to keep it on. Also, every time I leaned against the window, the makeup came off in tan circles and I had to clean the glass hurriedly before anyone noticed. After several hours on the bus, the wig started to slip and I found it to be a nuisance rather than charming. At a rest stop, I again went into the ladies' room, this time to take off the wig, fluff up my dark hair, wash off the makeup and put on sunglasses.

What I didn't realize was that I had been observed by an elderly lady on the bus. This woman had stared everyone down as they boarded the bus, daring them to sit next to her. She had carried her suitcases onto the bus with her, not trusting their care to anyone. As a single girl traveling alone I must have aroused her attention: more than once on the bus during the first part of the trip I had caught her looking at me. Now she was looking at me again. I hid behind a magazine.

The woman promptly went to the driver and accused me of doing something to "that girl with the blonde hair."

"See?" she said. "She even has that girl's clothes on!"

The driver took a long look at me standing in line, then all six feet of him sauntered over to my quivering form and asked for my identification and bus ticket. Embarrassed, I had to produce it, plus the blonde wig. He tried so hard not to laugh—as did everyone within a ten foot radius—but to no avail. For the rest of the bus trip I sat in the back, hiding behind a newspaper and wishing the bottom of the bus would open and swallow me.

I learned from this experience that God made me a special way and that's the way I was to be—me. *I* should make an appearance, not a blonde wig or heavy makeup. I realized that during this entire confrontation not one person had mentioned "acne." It had been a huge problem to me, but apparently to no one else.

My cousin, who was a budding actress, eventually used the blonde wig as a prop. During my visit with her, none of her friends ever mentioned my skin and I found myself relaxing and enjoying my vacation. I let go of the problem and left it in God's capable hands. Strange—when I returned home, my acne had almost disappeared.

And I'm still a brunette.

Marie Asner is a journalist in the Kansas City area. She is a workshop presenter and poet who won both the poetry competition and Grand Prize in writing at the 1998 Kansas City Christian Writers Network Conference.

Address: P.O. Box 4343, Overland Park, KS 66204-0343
Fax: (913) 385-5369.

## They Called Me AWOL

### Bob Hostetler

My mother died less than a month after I entered ninth grade. Then, on top of that traumatic experience, I had to move with my father to a new home three states away. At the same time, of course, I began attending a new high school—but only occasionally.

To say I had trouble focusing on school would be like saying the cyclops had trouble crossing his eye. I began to skip school so frequently I was branded with the nickname "AWOL" by my freshman biology teacher, Mr. Phillips. He would call my name in class and, when I didn't answer, would add the comment, "AWOL again." In my first two-and-a-half years of high school, I flunked all but one class.

I refined truancy to an art form. My father would drop me off at school each morning. I would enter the front door of the school, exit out the back and walk the several miles to the mobile home in which my father and I lived.

I became an expert at lying, forging absence excuses in my father's handwriting, falsifying report cards and creating clever-but-credible stories when school officials would call on the phone during the day (when my father was away at work). I screened the mail every day to filter anything that threatened to disrupt my career as a truant, and I reviewed the school lunch menus in the newspaper each week in case Dad would happen to ask what I'd had for lunch that day. I saved the lunch money he gave me every morning and used it at the end of the week to add to my music collection.

As month after month of this kind of behavior passed, I descended deeper into a frustrating cycle.

"I've had enough of this," I would resolve practically every Friday afternoon. I knew my life was going nowhere. I wasn't just flunking school, I was flunking life. I knew that the future looked pretty bleak for a kid with no high school diploma and few skills or talents other than deceiving his father.

While my friends were starting to make plans for college, I figured I'd still be taking freshman English in my early twenties. "I'm going back," I'd vow, "first thing Monday morning."

But despite my best intentions, week after week passed and the cycle continued.

I finally started going back to high school, but not because the school caught me or because my father threatened to ship me off to a military academy. I didn't even start attending school after my dad had to take me to juvenile court, where the judge threatened to throw my father in jail, send me to reform school and feed me to a bunch of hunger-crazed alligators (and not necessarily in that order).

The truth is, my girlfriend from church found out.

You see, the whole time I had been skipping school and lying to everyone who knew me, I had been acting like a "model Christian" at church—and had been dating the pastor's daughter! I remember the day she discovered the truth about my truancy.

I was visiting at her house when her father came into the room, accompanied by my oldest brother (my father was out of town at the time, and my adult brother, who lived nearby, was filling in for him). They suggested we go to a restaurant down the street to talk.

I went with them like a death-row prisoner being led to the execution chamber. To make a long story short (I know, it's too late for that), they informed me that my school-skipping days were over, and that I would have to submit to some rather strict requirements if I hoped to avoid a starring role on "Lifestyles of the Poor and Pathetic."

When I returned to my girlfriend's house, she was waiting for me, her eyes wide with curiosity. I told her everything.

"I haven't gone to school for over two years," I confessed. "I've been skipping school and lying to my father, and to you and to everyone else at church."

I expected her to drop me like a bad habit. But she didn't. She was pretty upset for a while, but once she cooled down she just let me know that her plans for the future did not include foraging in trash cans for food; she told me I'd better start attending high school.

It wasn't easy, but I did manage to kick my habit of playing hooky. I had a lot of catching up to do, of course, and it was often humiliating to sit through Freshman classes as a sixteen- and seventeen-year-old. I had to work harder once I started back; since I didn't want to wear a hearing aid and a pacemaker to my high school graduation, I had to cram as many classes as possible into my schedule.

I also had a reputation to redeem. I discovered that my truancy had earned me a reputation for trouble at school. I didn't just want to return to classes; I wanted to begin walking with God there—as well as at church. I wanted to stop living a double life and instead serve God at school as well as I had ever served Him at church.

It was hard and often discouraging—there's no doubt about that. I had a lot of work to make up and a lot of obstacles to overcome. But I learned to lean on God more than I ever had before, and He gave me more strength—and more success—

than I would have thought possible. I took one day at a time and was often amazed at how God got me through each day.

I finished high school only a year late. My girl-friend waited for me, and later became my wife. I even managed to earn a college degree and graduate with a perfect (4.0) grade point average. And, while I'm not endorsing truancy (my own children aren't allowed to miss school unless they have a note from God), God used my experiences for good. They formed the basis of my first novel and my sixth book to be published: *They Call Me AWOL* (Horizon Books, Camp Hill, Pennsylvania).

*They Call Me AWOL* is the story of Ben Howard, a "model Christian" teenager—at church. He attends church every Sunday, sings in the choir, teaches a Sunday school class and is dating Randi, the pastor's daughter. But things are different at school. He is called "AWOL" because of his habit of missing school more than he attends. One day, however, Ben's two lives come crashing together when Randi announces she's transferring to his school. In horror, Ben realizes he only has two weeks to bring his "two lives" into one or risk losing Randi.

The book is a novel, not an autobiography. Major events and elements of the book are ficticious, and some actual events were altered to make them funnier or more interesting. Despite the fact that it is a novel, *They Call Me*

*AWOL* incorporates many of my true experiences as a teenage truant.

For example, when I feared that the school would contact my father with an evening phone call, I employed the technique of disconnecting the cord at the back of the phone to prevent incoming calls—a technique Ben uses in the book.

Another true-to-life element is the wisecracking biology teacher who tags Ben with the nickname "AWOL."

Not long ago I called my former high school and set up a meeting with Larry Phillips, the biology teacher who had created my teenage nickname. He probably thought it was a joke— that I would once again go AWOL! As surprised as he may have been that I showed up at school that day (when I had failed to show up so often before), he appeared even more surprised when I presented him with an inscribed copy of the novel whose title he had unknowingly inspired.

When I told Mr. Phillips that not only had I written a novel based on my high school experience, but that God had also blessed me beyond my wildest dreams by giving me a rewarding ministry as a Christian author, his eyes filled with tears. Then he told me something I never knew: he was a Christian too and had sometimes prayed for me when I was a struggling high school student.

Mr. Phillips waited for his next class to finish filing into their seats, and then introduced me, briefly explaining what I had been like as a student, adding that I was now a best-selling and award-winning author.

"He was one of the brightest students I ever had," he said, "but I've never had one who seemed more hopeless." Then he clasped his arm around my shoulders and told the class, "If *he* can make it, *anybody* can!"

It wasn't exactly the best compliment I've ever received, but he was right. If, with God's help, I can bounce back from a cycle of hopelessness and failure, *anybody* can.

Bob Hostetler's books have sold nearly a million copies. In addition to *They Call Me AWOL,* they include the award-winning *Don't Check Your Brains at the Door* (co-authored with Josh McDowell) and *Holy Moses (And Other Adventures in Vertical Living).* He is also a frequent speaker at churches, conferences and retreats. He has been a disc jockey, pastor, magazine editor, freelance book editor and (with his wife Robin) a foster parent to ten teenage boys (though not all at once). He and Robin have two children, Aubrey and Aaron. They live in Hamilton, Ohio.

## "Beck the Wreck"

### Becki Conway Sanders

"Beck the Wreck" is my nickname, and I have always lived up to it. I am active and athletic—and accident prone. And so, three days before my fifteenth birthday, I was keeping a doctor's appointment for a dislocated tailbone I'd gotten while cheerleading.

While I was there I mentioned casually, "I've also got this problem with my left knee. Every so often it swells up and I limp around or use crutches for a few days; then the pain goes away. It's been going on for a couple of years."

The doctor didn't share my casual attitude; he insisted on taking an X ray. He discovered that six inches of the bone above my left knee was three times thicker than normal. He suggested that we contact an orthopedist immediately. I never expected *this* for my fifteenth birthday!

33

Dr. Scott Kline was an orthopedic surgeon new to our local clinic. We knew him because he attended our church. After his exam and more X rays, he told us I had a large tumor just above my knee. He wanted me hospitalized for a biopsy as soon as possible.

Dr. Kline was straightforward about the possibilities. He gently explained to us that the outcome might be serious. I might need a bone graft—or an amputation. Death was even a prospect.

As I heard the serious possibilities that day, God gave me an unusual peace about my future. I vowed to myself and God that I would make the best of it. When negative thoughts came—usually when I was out running or having fun with friends—I gave them to God and asked for His help with whatever happened.

After the biopsy, Dr. Kline remained uncertain about what type of tumor I had, but felt it probably was not malignant. He sent samples of the tumor to other labs and consulted many physicians and pathologists across the United States. The opinions from the consultations were inconclusive.

Meanwhile, God was preparing me for the future He knew I was to have. While I was recovering from the biopsy, I met Joni Eareckson Tada, who spoke at two meetings in our city. Sitting in her wheelchair, she used a pen in her mouth to draw a picture. One time, she drew a cabin in a beautiful mountain setting. When the drawing was nearly complete, she suddenly ruined the picture with two black lines through either side of the cabin.

I wondered, *What is she doing?*

Quickly she made her point: "Sometimes God allows dark lines to become part of our lives. But He uses those dark experiences to perfect us and help us grow into the people we wants us to be."

As she spoke, she transformed the two lines into beautiful pine trees that complemented and completed the picture. She talked about her experiences and all that God had taught her as a quadriplegic.

At the time it looked as if my tumor were benign, so I had no idea that I might go through something as life-changing and permanent as her experience. (See Joni's story on p. 93.) Still, I was struck by Joni's testimony. It was exciting that God had turned something so awful into a ministry that glorified Him and helped others.

After a second biopsy, Dr. Kline again sent samples to pathologists specializing in rare tumors. For the second time in over a year, I was told to wait.

During this waiting period, I met many people with handicaps. I talked with them and watched how they dealt with their disabilities and suffering. I sensed a bond with them and felt God had intentionally arranged for our paths to cross.

Dr. Kline was receiving mixed professional opinions about the tumor samples. We didn't know at the time how much he agonized over the possibilities, weighing all the pros and cons. Finally, with the counsel of many experts, he reluctantly decided on what he felt was the most medically sound course of action.

Strangely, when Dr. Kline explained the need for amputation, I had a number of feelings—shock, excitement, curiosity and peace. I'd had an underlying suspicion that it was coming, so the news wasn't totally unexpected. I didn't feel angry. In fact, I was relieved to finally know what was going to happen.

I also felt responsible to help my parents. They seemed totally destroyed by this news. I wanted to show them that I'd make it through this trial.

More than anything, I felt a deep responsibility to God. I sensed God was going to use me in special ways—that He was giving me a big opportunity—and I didn't want to lose it by being selfish or self-absorbed.

I had been asking God where He wanted me to go to college and what profession He wanted me to pursue. Now I felt that God was answering my prayer—maybe not in the way I thought He would, but in a distinct way all the same.

God was tailoring me for a specific service, one I might not have been able to do as well with a whole, healthy body. I now would be able to understand loss in other people's lives.

The morning I was being wheeled from my hospital room into surgery, my dad walked alongside holding my hand. Before he, Mom and my sisters had to say good-bye to me, Dad said, "Don't worry, honey. They're going to open up your leg and find that the cancer's gone."

I wanted to believe that for his sake, but I honestly didn't feel healing was God's plan for me. Instead I felt God's incredible strength and sensed a tremendous courage that I'd never previously possessed. I was sure God was in control and present with me every second.

Earlier, the nurses had asked me to "prep" the surgical area. I shaved my entire leg and scrubbed it for fifteen minutes to make it sterile. I looked at how tan, athletic and healthy that leg looked from the outside. I thanked God for all that He had given me, and then I said "good-bye" to my left leg.

The next thing I remember was waking up in terrible pain. I couldn't sit up to see if my left leg was there. I tried to move it. All I felt was incredible pain.

*OK, God, it really has happened,* I thought. *Here we go.*

God gave me a remarkably fast recovery and I progressed quickly in the physical therapy program so that in a couple of days I was walking on crutches, feeling relatively stable.

I walked around my hospital floor and looked in the rooms of the other patients, most of whom were cancer victims. I saw people who were suffering with great pain. I met a twelve-year-old girl who didn't have long to live. She and her family were devastated. As I compared my circumstances with those of other patients, I knew I was greatly blessed.

My first few days after surgery were not only a time for physical recovery but also for social adjustment. When my friends came into my hospital room, I sensed their discomfort. They wanted to encourage me, but my missing leg distressed them. They knew that, physically, I was permanently changed.

Many of my friends were afraid my amputation would alter my personality. When they came to visit me, they would awkwardly look out the window, or at the cards and flowers—anywhere but the vacant spot on my bed. They stood around, not knowing what to do or say. So I joked with them or invited them to sit down on the empty side of the bed.

They seemed surprised to find me cheerful and involved in life. Often I made wisecracks about what a great diet I was on: "Look, I lost seventeen pounds in three hours." Or I'd joke about the hospital expenses: "You know, it costs an arm and a leg to be in here, but the insurance covered the arm."

I needed to be an educator to the able-bodied people around me. I had been "normal" for sixteen years and I knew how I had perceived disabled people. I could remember being uncomfortable around people in wheelchairs or on crutches. Now that I was on the other side of the fence, I could help able-bodied people understand that disabled people are normal, with struggles similar to their own.

Some of my friends had ignored the spiritual side of me because they weren't Christians. After I lost my leg, they began to say, "You're different. Why aren't you reacting to your amputation like I would?"

They listened as I told them about my faith in Jesus Christ and that I was living for something much more lasting than what I was physically.

I knew God had answered prayers for my healing. He *had* healed me—emotionally. Incredibly, I never experienced serious depression or anger over my amputation. This was incredible to me and unbelievable to everyone else! Only my family and close friends knew I wasn't acting. People from the very first day tried to tell me I was in denial. People urged me to "get in touch with my feelings." I was—and my feelings were fine!

I knew this attitude was God's doing, because I know myself! I don't usually say, "OK, praise the Lord and pass the potatoes!" I usually give God a fight before I yield to His ultimate power and authority. The peace I felt was an extraordinary reaction for me.

Shortly after my surgery, I had to choose a book for an English class report. Since I had been impressed by Joni when I met her in person, I decided to read her autobiography. Her attitudes strongly molded the way I dealt with my disability. I thought, *If I can learn from her times of anger and depression, maybe I won't go through all of that. Maybe I can skip to where her life was at the end of the book, when she could see God using her disability.*

I realized my disability couldn't compare to her quadriplegia, but I saw that her attitudes applied to my situation. Her life dramatically affected mine, especially in how she wanted to praise the Lord by everything she did.

In my senior year of high school, I met my first recreation therapist while I was learning to ski as an amputee in Colorado. She was my ski instructor. I began to think this would be the perfect career for me. I enjoyed people and was able to do many sports. Besides, I was academically sound in the sciences I would need for a recreation therapy degree.

My disability would be an additional "perk" for understanding the people I'd be working with. I had learned that sports and recreation enable people to feel "normal."

I planned to attend a Christian college for a couple of years and then transfer to a state school to finish the specific requirements of my degree. While I was getting used to college life, the other students were getting used to me. Many of them told me I was the first handicapped friend they had ever had.

Besides people like Joni, another important role model for me was Sandy, my college roommate. To look at Sandy, most people would think she was a normal, healthy young woman, but she had a chronic intestinal illness, Crohns' disease, which was diagnosed when she was only eight years old. Some days her abdominal pain was so bad she couldn't get out of bed.

Sandy taught me not to use suffering as an excuse. She never complains. When people look at me they see I am disabled. They give me support and encouragement. When people look at Sandy, they don't see any problem. They don't realize that Sandy, and the other "Sandys" of the world with hidden illnesses, are heroic and courageous in the way they live.

It's one thing to go through traumatic surgery and the terror of cancer while people applaud and say, "Good job, well done!" It's harder to wear an artificial leg every day and put up with backaches, blisters on my stump and getting fatigued because of the energy it takes to propel the leg. Everyday difficulties are more tiring, in some ways, than the initial loss. God used Sandy to teach me how to live life for God's glory without complaining and to look beyond myself and my pain to other people's needs.

God was getting me ready to care for other people who have illnesses and disabilities. Perhaps I have more understanding and compassion toward my patients than an able-bodied person might have. If so, it's because I have been there. I know what it feels like.

A few months after my amputation, a nurse from our church called me about Calvin, a sixteen-year-old patient of hers. He had just had a leg amputated because of cancer and was so depressed he wouldn't talk. My nurse friend asked if I would visit him in the hospital.

I walked into Calvin's room and introduced myself. He barely looked up until he saw that I was on one leg.

"It looks like you and I have something in common," I ventured. "I see by the lump under your sheets that it's even the same leg."

He seemed horrified that I mentioned the lump, but I went on, "I used to call mine a basketball. But don't worry, the swelling eventually goes down. I'm waiting now for my stump to heal enough to get fitted with a fake leg."

Eventually he shared that not only had he avoided looking at his stump, but he hadn't discussed the loss of his leg with anyone. Calvin had also decided to drop out of life. Although he was a good student, he didn't plan to return to school. When I told him he would still be able to drive a car because he had his right leg, he said his family's cars all had manual transmissions—"You need two legs to drive them." He didn't care anyway; there was no place to go and no one he wanted to see.

I could tell this guy needed a new perspective, so I prayerfully worked at helping him. He needed to grieve the loss of his leg. He also needed to accept the fact that life would be different, but he would still be able to do many things.

During my visits, Calvin began to feel free to talk about his situation. His depression lifted. He could look at his stump and acknowledge that his leg was actually gone. He began to think of things he wanted to do. He talked about getting his dad to buy a car with an automatic transmission. He decided to go back to school.

One day as I left his room, his parents were coming down the hall. They thanked me over and over for how I had helped Calvin find hope.

"I'm glad I could," I said, "but I just passed on the encouragement that God and other people gave me."

Experiencing pain teaches us how to comfort others and help them trust "the God of all comfort, who comforts us in all our troubles, so that we can comfort those in any trouble with the comfort we ourselves have received from God" (2 Corinthians 1:3-4).

From *Trusting God in a Family Crisis* by Becki Conway Sanders, Jim and Sally Conway. © 1989 Becki Conway Sanders, Jim and Sally Conway. Used by permission.

Becki Conway Sanders was born in Newton, Kansas, the daughter of a pastor and youngest of three daughters. She worked for several years in Recreation Therapy in Rehabilitation hospitals in Southern California. Becki and her husband, Craig Sanders, pastor of North Park Fellowship Presbyterian Church, live with their three daughters near Boise, Idaho. She is an instructor for an adaptive snow skiing program and runs a home business.

# The Majesty of Grace

## Dennis Jernigan

At an early age, I became involved in sexual immorality (homosexuality), which enveloped my being well into young adulthood. The reasons were many. Suffice it to say, I had a warped understanding of God. My father was not openly affectionate toward me. He was a good provider and always present in my life—I just never heard him verbally express love or approval of me; I only heard the verbal expressions of how I failed him.

As a result I came to believe it was my performance that would make me acceptable and pleasing to him. My life became one long obsession to gain his love and approval. The need for fatherly approval became intertwined with my sexual identity and resulted in perversion.

I simply believed a lot of lies from a very early age—lies about my father and lies about myself. Looking back, it is very easy to see that many

45

and constant were my father's expressions of love for me; I just did not see them at the time. I have now learned the truth; but more importantly, I have "put on" that truth.

I discovered that God had gifted me musically—so much so that I was the church pianist from the time I was nine years old. I was often called a "sissy" and had all other manner of insults heaped upon me—insults that are often placed upon a little boy who happens to play the piano.

I knew that what I struggled with sexually was a sin. I just did not know how to overcome it at the time. I often heard "church people" talk about what needed to be done with homosexuals—like ship them all out of the country—and I heard them say that all homosexuals belonged in hell. Hearing this from my elders, I felt I had no place to go for help. The church was the *last* place I felt I could go. The *world* sounded more loving and accepting.

My resultant conclusion was that God was like my perception of my father and the church—unapproachable, harsh and totally disgusted with who I was.

After college, my life came crashing to the bottom. The Lord met me there with the love and forgiveness I had only dreamed about. He led me into the deepest intimacy I have ever known.

The fact that He allowed me to know Him and to be known by Him—and the realization that I have not even begun to tap into the full extent of all He is—this is the epitome of majesty to me. He cleansed me of my sin with His redeeming blood and filled my life with overcoming grace—so much grace that I am a married man and the father of nine children; so much redemption that my father now works with me in my ministry to others!

Father God has taken me on an incredible journey of discovery—a discovery of His great depths and, along the way, a discovery of who I am. He continues to redeem my past in ways I never thought possible. There were many times in my life when my perception was that God had abandoned me. But as I have sought to know Him, I have come to realize that He can even redeem those old memories of abandonment by revealing to me *His* perspective on those situations and circumstances.

A few years ago, I took a worship team back to minister in the town where I grew up. After the service, an older woman approached me with these words: "Isn't it wonderful how your grandmother's prayers for you have been answered?" My grandmother had died when I was twelve years old, and I had no memories of any prayers for me.

I told the woman, "I have no idea what you are talking about. But would you please tell me?"

She asked me if I remembered the times—almost daily—when I would go to my grandmother's house and play the piano. I told her that I did, indeed, remember those precious times. She then told me that whenever I would play the piano at her house, my Grandmother Jernigan would stand behind me and pray for me—she prayed that God would use me in the area of worship and music for His glory!

I was overwhelmed with joy and gratitude as I thought about all that God had done in my life. Immediately, the Holy Spirit reminded me of all the times, even as a twelve-year-old, when I felt that God had forsaken me. But now He gently said, "See, I was there all the time. I loved you so much that I even had others praying for you, and you didn't even know it."

What joy! What a loving God! What *majesty!*

From *A Mystery of Majesty,* © 1997 by Dennis Jernigan. All rights reserved. Howard Publishing Co., Inc., West Monroe, LA. Used by permission.

*Photo courtesy of Shepherd's Heart.*

Dennis Jernigan is a worship leader and composer whose deeply sensitive praise and worship songs have such inspirational impact that he has been called "the spiritual psalmist for the twentieth century." In 1983, he married Melinda Hewitt, and together they have nine children. For over fifteen years, his ministry has centered on the promise of God's powerfully simple truth—that His mercy is for everyone, regardless of mistakes and shortcomings of the past.

# A New Song for Claudia

## Claudia Russell Ward

When I was eighteen, I headed for *La Scala*, the renowned opera house of Milan, Italy. My traveling companions were Mrs. B, a psychic medium, and her daughter, Mary. The only thing we had in common was the world of opera, which was why we decided to go to *La Scala* together to study.

I was relieved to be leaving California because I feared I might be pregnant. For the past three years I had lived a promiscuous lifestyle along with being hooked on drugs and alcohol. I knew this was a disastrous combination, but I couldn't stop. If in fact I was pregnant, I planned to have an abortion in Italy—that way no one would know! I had heard that any kind of surgery in Europe was risky, but the fear of having a child all alone in a foreign country terrified me even more.

I tried to forget my troubles during the trip, hoping things would get better once I reached Italy. But it was in Italy where my troubles truly began.

It rained incessantly and my companions and I discovered that finding good coaches and voice teachers was a constant problem.

The worst part was that Mrs. B and her daughter blamed me for all our bad luck. They were convinced my influence was "evil," so without any concern for me, they said "*addio*" and departed for Germany.

On the other side of the world from home, alone, ignorant of the language and the culture, I was grateful for just one thing: I wasn't pregnant.

I stayed in Milan for three years. News from home was always sad; my father was dying from alcoholism and my parents were about to lose the family drugstore, but I tried not to think about it. Eventually I found a wonderful voice teacher, learned the language, memorized four of Puccini's operas and enjoyed *la dolce vita* (the sweet life) for a while. But in the depths of my soul I was still in agony.

Camille, a boyfriend from Calabria, invited me to visit Rome with him. Standing in front of the Fountain of Trevi, I threw a coin in and wished for success. *Why do I feel so empty and sad?* I wondered. *I'm doing well and yet I don't re-*

*ally know why I'm living or what the purpose of my
life is. What is the answer, God?*

I had called out to God once before, on a very
dark night in San Diego when I was seventeen. I
was so drunk I nearly drowned in San Diego
Bay, but someone pulled me out. While I was re-
cuperating I prayed for the first time in my life. I
knew I was going to die if I didn't turn around. I
asked God to help me find Him, wherever He
was. Somehow, I had forgotten about that simple prayer. Now, here I was again at another
crossroads, offering another prayer.

When I returned to Milan, the answer to that
prayer began to unfold. Doris, a tall, slim New
Yorker who was also studying opera, entered my
life. We both lived in the same hotel on the same
floor, and one day she just walked into my room.
As we got to know one another, she decided to
make me her "mission." She was determined to
introduce me to an American couple who lived
in Switzerland. Like a broken record she would
say, "They will tell you the true meaning of
Christianity." (Like I cared!)

Her persistence finally paid off, and I agreed
to go to Switzerland with her to stay with her
weird friends. They lived in a chalet high in the
Swiss Alps. Their names were Edith and Francis
Schaeffer (yes, the renowned evangelical Christian theologian) and their home was called
*L'Abri* (The Shelter).

Students and people of varied nationalities
filled their home, most of them seeking some

kind of rationale for living. After a few days I was a nervous wreck—I would have given anything for a smoke and a drink, but I couldn't pull it off in such a sterile environment.

But as time went on, I began to mellow in my attitude. What had seemed a cloying atmosphere filled with so much "God-talk" began to warm into a spirit of love and caring. I came to admire Dr. Schaeffer; I was impressed by his brilliance and his sincerity, though his words still baffled me.

Finally, I met Dr. Schaeffer face-to-face at the breakfast table. He shocked me with a very blunt question: "Tell me, Claudia, when did you become a Christian?"

I had no idea what he meant. I told him about being addicted to drugs and alcohol, and about the past I had been living. We talked for three hours that morning about what the Bible says in regard to man and his connection to God, the Creator. He explained that our sin separates us from God, who is holy, but that God has provided for us a way back to Him through His Son, Jesus Christ. Finally he asked me if I believed that Jesus died for *me*, Claudia.

I was still dubious. "I'll have to think about that. Nobody loves *me* that much!" I replied. I got up and started to head for the door, but something Dr. Schaeffer said pulled me back.

"Yes, He does," Dr. Schaeffer replied gently. "In Romans 5:8 the Bible says that 'while we were still sinners, Christ died for us.' Are you ready to believe that Jesus Christ loved you so much that He died for *your* sins, so *you* could have a relationship with God?"

My past flashed before me. I thought of the times I had prayed for God to show me the way out of my depths of despair and degradation. Could this be the answer to those prayers?

"I don't know what is happening here," I told him, "but my heart wants to say *'yes.'* "

As I said it, a sense of forgiveness and peace swept over me. I let go of my past and invited Christ into my heart. As I did, I actually heard bells ring; peace flooded my soul, and life finally, for the first time, had meaning. The searching prayers I had prayed were answered.

"You need to thank your heavenly Father," Dr. Schaeffer said.

"How do I do that?"

"Just bow your head and the Holy Spirit will give you the words."

And He did. I thanked God for my forgiveness and then prayed, "Take my life, Lord, and I will follow You."

What a struggle my teenage years had been—but I made it through. Departing from Europe on the *Queen Mary* was a complete contrast to my prior voyage when I left New York harbor the first time. Looking out over the vast ocean, I rejoiced over its majesty. I now knew the One who made each wave and all the creatures in it. I couldn't get enough of God's Word, and each day I would remember the scripture that Dr. Schaeffer had shared with me at *L'Abri*.

Isaiah 54 verses 4 and 5 say: "Do not be afraid . . . . You will forget the shame of your youth. . . . For your Maker is your husband—the LORD Almighty is his name—the Holy One of Israel is your Redeemer." No matter what my marital status would be in this world, I would always be married to the Lord.

The world of opera was over for me, but God put into my heart a new song—a song that will live on forever.

Claudia Russell Ward lives in El Cajon, California, near San Diego, with her husband Hal. They have four adult children and six grandchildren. Claudia is active as a conference speaker, composer, playwright, performer and writer. She has written for a number of publications and has composed two children's musicals. She is active in the Christian Community Theater of San Diego.

Address: 11466 Fuertes Farms Road, El Cajon, CA 92020.

# Grateful for Grace

## Jerry B. Jenkins

When I was in elementary school, my dad once took my brothers and me to the home of a crotchety old man who said that one of us had thrown a rock through his window.

I had not done it, but all the way to the man's house, fear gripped me. What if he said he had seen me? Would my father believe me? I knew I would look and sound guilty.

"If you didn't do it, you have nothing to fear," Dad said. "No one can be hurt by the truth."

True enough, but any one of us could have been hurt by an old man who mistook us for someone else.

"Tell me which one did it," my dad told the man, "and we'll make it right."

The man studied our faces and admitted he had been mistaken. The ride home was much more pleasant.

A few years later, when I was a high school freshman, I was unjustly accused. But this time I was at school, dealing with an angry, beefy football coach, and my dad was not there as a mediator. Although I was innocent, I felt scared and guilty.

I had broken my arm during one of the first few weeks of freshman football practice. I watched the rest of the season in a cast, but grew bored hanging around. So I helped the equipment managers. It wasn't my assignment. I could come and go as I pleased. It was just something to do.

When someone left a mess of wet towels in the locker room one day, the coach exploded. To avoid that ex-military man and his legendary five-foot paddle—which he swung with both hands and which had launched more than one malcontent headfirst into the lockers—the real equipment managers somehow succeeded in laying the blame at my feet. I learned this as I innocently walked in on the scene.

Picture a beet-red coach and several pale, quaking managers.

"Grab your ankles, Jenkins," the coach bellowed. "I'll teach you to leave a mess like this."

I protested that I wasn't even a manager, that I was an injured player, but that I would be happy to clean it up anyway. I searched the eyes of my accusers and knew they were only protecting their own hides.

The coach didn't stall. "Grab 'em!"

Only my left arm reached the ankle. My right hung suspended, bent rigid in plaster. Upside down, I could see between my knees the coach sweeping back that gigantic paddle. I heard the whoosh and saw the wide eyes of the guilty. I shut my eyes and tried not to tighten. The paddle stopped inches from my seat, and the coach tapped me ever so lightly with it. He smiled. "You're not a manager." he said. "You are an injured player!"

I nearly collapsed with relief. When the coach ordered the managers to line up for their punishment, I quickly cleaned up the wet towels. There's something about a reprieve that makes one benevolent, even when the punishment would have been unjust.

I have been unjustly accused a few other times. I hurt the worst when my motives are questioned or when I am accused of lying. If I support an unpopular decision, I may be charged with a personal vendetta. That can cause deep pain.

All such experiences force me to think of the grossest case of unjust accusation in history, when a Man who knew no sin became sin for us, that we might become the righteousness of God in Him (2 Corinthians 5:21). Not only had He done no wrong, but He was righteousness personified. And not only was He wrongly accused, He was also put to death.

Thinking about the ultimate sacrifice by the epitome of innocence puts our puny trials into perspective. And realizing that Jesus died on our behalf in spite of our unworthiness should also affect our self-images. Rather than impressing us with ourselves, it should leave us grateful for grace.

> From *Life Flies When You're Having Fun* by Jerry B. Jenkins. © 1993 Jerry B. Jenkins. Used by permission.

Jerry B. Jenkins, a former Vice President of Publishing at Moody Bible Institute and Editor of *Moody* magazine, has authored more than 100 books, including the best-selling "Left Behind" series co-authored with Tim LaHaye. His writing has appeared in *Reader's Digest, Parade* and dozens of Christian periodicals. He has written numerous biographies, including books with Hank Aaron, Bill Gaither and Nolan Ryan. He assisted Billy Graham with his memoirs, *Just As I Am.* He also writes *Gil Thorpe*, a nationally syndicated sports comic strip. Jerry and his wife and three sons live in Zion, IL.

Address: Alive Communications Literary Agency, Suite 329, 1465 Kelly Johnson Blvd., Colorado Springs, CO 80920.

# A Weekend to Remember

## Karen O'Connor

"I'm afraid," I told myself before a trip to my friend's house. "What if we get in a car accident?"

"I'm afraid," I whispered in bed at night. "What if I don't wake up?"

"I'm afraid," I wrote in my diary. "What if Dad really does have a weak heart and he dies before I grow up?"

Fear followed me throughout my growing up years—until one special weekend in August, 1951 at Girl Scout Camp. I was thirteen years old at the time.

On Saturday morning our leader said we could tromp through the creek as long as we wore our rubber boots to keep from cutting our feet on the rocks. The other girls donned their boots and jumped right in. I stood back, watching—and wishing I had their courage. I looked at the water rushing downstream and was instantly afraid I'd be swept away.

Next, we were told we could use our knives to whittle a twig into a piece of sculpture. I was afraid I'd cut my hand.

I was afraid to help build the bonfire. I was afraid to perform in a skit. I was afraid to lead the group in song, even though I had a nice voice. No matter what occurred, I had some reservation about it.

That evening when I crawled into my bedroll, I feared waking in the night to go to the creepy old outhouse at the end of a long dark path behind the lodge. It had a hornet's nest in the corner and there was no light inside. I felt restless all night, tossing and turning in concern. I wanted so much to be a real part of this weekend, to put away the fear and shyness that kept me separated from the other girls. But I didn't know how to do it.

Then, just as I had feared, I woke up in the middle of the night. I knew I wouldn't be able to hold out till morning; I'd have to take that dreaded path to the dark outhouse.

I wiggled out of the bedroll and slipped into my sandals, trying not to awaken anyone around me. My heart raced.

Then, suddenly, a gentle hand touched my shoulder.

"Karen, is anything wrong? Can I help?" It was our leader, Mrs. Quinn. I burst into tears at the sound of her voice.

"I have to go to the bathroom," I sobbed. "But I'm scared to go alone."

"Of course. I understand," she said softly. "I'm scared too. In fact, I need to make a trip there as well. Why don't we go together?"

Mrs. Quinn grabbed her flashlight with one hand and my hand with the other, and off we went. A feeling of peace and calm came over me during that short walk. The stars sparkled and crickets chirped softly in the darkness. A sliver of a moon shone overhead and a cool breeze wafted through our nightgowns. In that moment, fear evaporated like raindrops in a summer wind.

After we returned, Mrs. Quinn made sure I was safely tucked in and then she planted a warm kiss on my forehead and said, "God bless you. Sleep tight."

I did sleep tight the rest of that night. I woke up with a new freedom and confidence I had not known before. I made the most of that last day at camp, joining others in the stream and perching myself on a sturdy branch to whittle a piece of wood with my new knife.

I had bounced back from fear and I knew it would never grip me again in the same way. Mrs. Quinn had given me her hand when I most needed it. That experience led me to reach out for other hands along the way and eventually to discover the power of the one hand that can keep me safe from fear forever—the hand of God.

I still have fearful moments, but I no longer hang back and allow fear to overwhelm me. I turn and face it, confident in the One who promised to be my strength and my shield.

> *For I am the LORD, your God,*
> *who takes hold of your right hand*
> *and says to you, Do not fear;*
> *I will help you. (Isaiah 41:13)*

Karen O'Connor is an award-winning author and a speaker specializing in personal and professional growth topics. She is author of thirty-five books, most recently, *Basket of Blessings: 31 Days to a More Grateful Heart* (WaterBrook Press). Karen has been on national radio and television and is a presenter for businesses, schools, churches and professional organizations.

E-mail: WordyKaren@aol.com

# The Neglected Art of Being Different

## Arthur Gordon

*Do not be conformed to this world but be transformed by the renewal of your mind, that you may prove what is the will of God, what is good and acceptable and perfect.*

(Romans 12:2, RSV)

One of the most vivid and painful recollections of my life concerns . . . a hat.

When I was a boy, my parents sent me to a summer camp run along semimilitary lines. Part of each camper's uniform was supposed to be a Boy Scout hat—low-crowned, wide-brimmed—to be worn every afternoon without fail when we lined up for formal inspection.

But my parents did not provide me with a scout hat. Through some catastrophic oversight, they sent me off with one of those army campaign hats,

63

vintage of 1917. It was wide-brimmed, all right: When I put it on, I was practically in total darkness. As for the crown, instead of being flat, it seemed to me to rise half a mile straight up in the air. Whenever I wore this hat, instead of being an inconspicuous and somewhat homesick kid, I became a freak.

Or so I thought. Looking back now, across the years, I can smile at the memory of my wan little face peering out forlornly from under that monstrosity of a hat. But it was no joke at the time. I was miserable—utterly, abjectly miserable. Why? Because I was *different,* different from the others, different from the crowd.

There must be few of us who cannot recall from some such childhood episode the loneliness and terror of being different. And fewer still who do not carry some of this deep-rooted fear into adult life. It's a fear as fundamental as the fear of falling, and in a sense it *is* a fear of falling—of falling out of favor with other people by differing from them. But if we value leadership, if we prize achievement, if we are concerned with our own painful struggle toward maturity, we have to learn to overcome this fear—or at least to control it.

The rewards of differentness are easy enough to see. No matter what field you choose—science, entertainment, law, education, the business world—the demand is for individuals whose performance is above average and therefore different. At any dinner party, the liveliest and most attractive guest is the one whose ideas and observations are stimulating because they are different. I have no doubt that if a survey were taken, the earning power of any given person would be found to parallel almost exactly his capacity to produce new ideas, to show unusual persistence or energy, to take chances—in other words, to be different.

The fear of being different, like most fears, tends to diminish when you drag it into the light and take a good look at it. At the bottom of such fear lies an intense preoccupation with self. That comical hat, back in my childhood, might have caused some momentary merriment or temporary teasing, but the whole thing was too trivial to have lasted long. I was the one who kept it alive by agonizing about it. Recognize this sort of self-consciousness as a form of inverted egotism, and you are not so likely to be victimized by it.

It also helps to remind yourself occasionally that some of the disapproval or hostility that you shrink from encountering is probably imaginary. This tendency to see menace where none exists afflicts us all to some extent and certainly begins early. We had a classic example the other day in our backyard. A visiting four-year-old encountered a small but lively cricket and yelled for help in piercing tones.

Our own three-year-old was very scornful about the whole thing. "Crickets don't hurt anybody," she said loftily. "I like crickets."

But the visitor was not to be cheated out of her fear so easily. "Crickets," she said with gloomy conviction, "don't like *me.*"

Another way to minimize the fear of being different is to remind yourself, if you really do run into resentment or ridicule, that you are in pretty good company. Very few of the great pioneers of thought or action escaped being laughed at, criticized or even martyred.

Most of the great religious leaders of history have been nonconformists. Christ was a religious revolutionist. He defied authority, as when He healed sick people on the Sabbath. He upset convention, as when He sat down to dinner with publicans and sinners. . . .

It takes courage to be different, but there is also an art to it—the art of not antagonizing people unnecessarily by your differentness. People don't object to differentness nearly as much as they object to the attitude of superiority that so often goes with it.

The rule of thumb is very simple: Be as different as you like, but try to be tolerant of the people who differ from you. If we all granted to one another the right simply to be ourselves, we would be different enough. When he was eight years old, someone asked Henry Thoreau what he was going to be when he grew up. "Why," said the boy, "I will be I!" He was, too.

So take a look at your life and check the areas where you are letting a foolish fear of "what people might say" hold you down or hold you back. Then go ahead and do a few of these unorthodox things. The penalties will certainly be less—and the rewards may be much greater—than you think.

From *A Touch of Wonder,* by Arthur Gordon. Fleming H. Revell, a division of Baker Book House Company, © 1974. Used by permission.

Arthur Gordon's writing celebrates "the small stuff" and points out the "endless free gifts that life offers." His journalistic career has spanned several decades and includes being an editor at *Reader's Digest, Ladies Home Journal* and *Guideposts* magazines. He lives in Savannah, Georgia.

## The Truth Set Me Free

## Lynn D. Morrissey

I was twenty years old and desperate. I had thought "growing out of" my depressing, suicidal teens would guarantee automatic happiness—but I was wrong.

As a teenager, I had rejected my Christian upbringing, frantically searching for truth in other belief systems and self-help concepts. I was hopelessly confused by conflicting philosophies I'd encountered. I suffered severe depression and longed to develop a plan for living to ensure peace and fulfillment. But truth was still elusive and now, at twenty, I had reached a dead end.

I wrote the following introduction in a document I titled "Life Plan":

> I am twenty years old and should be happy and ambitious, ready to embark into womanhood with assurance and poise, eager to savor life's joys. Yet I'm paranoid—afraid my hidden potentials

lie so far buried, they'll never appear. If I plunge soulfully into a quest for truth and happiness and fail to find them, I'm terrified of the emotional results!

I have gnawing conflicts over God. I've kept Him at arm's length as a last resort, afraid I won't find Him. I've tried desperately to suppress suicide on the chance of eventual contentment. Before I completely give up, maybe I'll ask God's help. If He's there, I'll be redeemed. If not, it doesn't matter anyway. I don't want to die if I can be happy. Death still might not be the best choice, yet if something doesn't change it will be my only choice.

I penned those anguished insights halfway through a ten-year period of suicidal depression lasting from my mid-teens to mid-twenties. Praise God, something did change! I turned to God and found salvation in Jesus Christ. He dramatically transformed me from a troubled teen, perilously poised on death's brink, to a stable woman whose life He infused with purpose.

I thought I had received Christ as a child. Raised by Christian parents, I attended church and Sunday school and memorized Scripture. At eleven, I predictably "went forward," believing that I had become a Christian. Yet I realize now I wasn't a Christian at all—I didn't have a personal relationship with Christ or a changed life. I rarely prayed or read my Bible, and when I did it was incomprehensible.

I lived a "fairy-tale '50s" childhood, and life in the '60s was similarly idyllic. Initially excelling in high school, I made honors grades, garnered leads in school musicals and enjoyed a relative state of popularity. Convinced my talents were exceptional, my flagrant arrogance disguised itself as self-confidence. Such self-centeredness obscured any need for God. I planned to attend college, become a French teacher, get married and live happily ever after.

Yet gradually, Camelot crumbled. Almost imperceptibly, I lost confidence in my abilities, personality and beliefs, ultimately becoming severely depressed. A once outgoing, happy teenager, I withdrew into a painful, immobilizing shell of shyness, finding it impossible to communicate with even family and intimate friends. I remember thinking I'd never have a normal conversation again. I grew so paranoid I'd sit in bathroom stalls until after classes began and would leave classes early to avoid talking to anyone. I became so debilitatingly depressed that I slept incessantly, regularly skipped classes and could barely study. My once "A and honors" grades plummeted to C's and D's.

Not only did I hate myself, but I also hated others for being everything I was not. Anger, bitterness and jealousy poisoned my thinking. Suicidal thoughts overwhelmed me. Although I never attempted to take my life, every day for literally ten

years I longed that it would end. Hopelessness en-
gulfed me.

What made me most hopeless was the disinte-
gration of my belief in God. I'd always thought I
could rely on God—that He was "out there"
somewhere—a "backup" solution to problems, a
surefire "last resort." But my search for truth, cou-
pled with a close friend's atheistic influence, convinced me God didn't exist.

Blessedly, God provided another friend, His
special angel, with whom I became reacquainted
after high school. Barbara was a Christian whose
incessant talk about Jesus had always intrigued
me. When she prayed, she was speaking with an
intimate Friend—real, but invisible. Her prayers
infused me with hope.

At this time, my mother's friend invited me to
attend a parachurch organization called Bible
Study Fellowship. Ironically, in my search for
truth, I'd never studied the Bible. I decided to
go with an open mind to discover if the Bible
were true.

I eagerly began reading the Bible daily, increasingly becoming aware of God's existence.
Everything the Bible revealed resonated deeply
within me as true. God was absolutely holy; I
was absolutely sinful. My only hope for reconciliation with God was to receive His Son, Jesus
Christ, as Lord and Savior because He was crucified to pay the penalty for my sin.

As a girl I was aware of these facts, but I hadn't
*owned* them. I'd also never personally confessed

my sinfulness or, by a deliberate act of my will, repented and asked Jesus to save me.

Then one evening when depression and self-hatred consumed me, I collapsed by my couch, sobbing convulsively, filled with guilt. Through self-reliant arrogance I'd rejected God and made a complete mess of my life. I no longer wanted any part of self-control. I surrendered to the Lord, asking Him to forgive my sins and rule my life.

Miraculously, the suffocating depression that had mercilessly oppressed me for ten years lifted. Within months I became outgoing and communicative. Anger, selfishness and jealousy melted as I reached out in compassion and love to others.

A "new person," I became increasingly dependent on God and constantly sought His will. I developed an insatiable hunger for God's Word and studied it daily, growing increasingly intimate with Him through a daily prayer journal. I fell head over heels in love with God, whose existence I had previously doubted.

Because I was spending more time in God's presence, the Holy Spirit radically changed my personality, helping me abandon unsavory habits and sins. I soon stopped cursing, wearing provocative clothing and watching immoral television and movies. With God's strength, I overcame my addiction to alcohol.

The Lord also overcame my fears and led me to a job which, amazingly, I held with regular attendance. I no longer hid in bathroom stalls, but easily communicated with people, advancing in my work until I was appointed as executive director of the USO agency in St. Louis.

Now the teenager who thought she would never find her potential or have a normal conversation again has become the woman who speaks and writes professionally for a living!

Suicide *is not* an option. Depressing teenage years without God need not be the end of a melancholy song. They can be the prelude to realizing your need for God, finding Him, receiving salvation and singing joyfully in God's presence forever!

 Lynn Morrissey communicates biblical concepts and personal strategies for Christian living through her *Words of Life* ministry, a combination of speaking, writing and conference outreach. A graduate of CLASS (Christian Leaders and Speakers Seminars), Precept Ministries Bible Study and Bible Study Fellowship, Lynn has been published in several devotional anthologies and in Christian magazines including *Today's Christian Woman* and *The Christian Communicator*.

Address: 155 Linden Avenue, St. Louis, MO 63105
E-mail: lynnswords @primary.net

## Never Give Up!

### Vincent Muli Wa Kituku

"Muli, you will repeat Standard Seven."

Those devastating words came from my father. His voice and his facial expression affirmed that my fate was sealed. His decisions were always final. I sat there saying nothing, but my tears said everything. My soul was wounded, my future blurred.

It was on a Saturday in January, 1974, when the results for the high school entrance exams were announced. I had not done well enough after completing Standard Seven (Kenya's equivalent to America's seventh grade). I had only a "C" average, and thus I couldn't be admitted to a government high school.

My uncle and my father's foster son, both my classmates, had better grades and both were admitted into good schools. Now my *younger brother* would become my classmate. This was a nightmare! He was three years younger than me and was the best student in his class—what we called an "academic sharpshooter." I hated to be humiliated by his excellent performance.

I hid myself in back of our house and cried, "Oh, God . . . why am I the only one who has to repeat?"

My mother, who had not seen me for hours, called my name. When I responded, she came and found me in my hiding place. With her arm on my shoulder, she said, "It is just one year, and then you can go to a good high school. My child, do not give up."

Why would I not give up? This was not the first time I was told to repeat a class. I had repeated second and sixth grades. Those earlier times were not so humiliating: I wasn't shown up by my relatives; I didn't have to be in the same class with my younger brother; and in those situations my fate was not determined by exams—my father had made those decisions on his own.

Besides, repeating Standard Seven was not a guarantee that I would get good grades. I knew neighbors who had sat for this high school entrance exam for seven years without succeeding.

When my mother left me alone, her words *"My child, do not give up,"* kept coming into my mind. Accustomed to reciting prayers that were written in a church book, I had never prayed from my heart. However, this time I prayed from my heart. I promised God that I would pray, attend church and study for the high school exam.

This childlike resolution consoled my heart. With rekindled hope, I repeated Standard Seven. Yes, my younger brother *did* perform better than I did—several times better. Other people made jokes about my academic abilities, but I did not let their opinion about me become *my* reality. I hit the books harder than ever before, prayed and attended church as regularly as I could.

Not long before the exam date, I suffered from malaria. I thought this would be the end of my dream of ever joining government high school. But God had everything planned—I was relatively well when it came time to sit for the exams. When the exam results were announced in January, 1975, I had an average of "B," and I was admitted to Tala High School. My brother and I were two of about ten students from a class of 120 who were admitted to government high schools.

Four years later, I was admitted to a two-year advanced level high school after another international exam that forced thousands of students out of their dreams for further education.

After those two years, I sat for the university entrance exam. This was known as an "exterminator." For every hundred students, less than ten made it to the university.

Again, I made it.

It was while attending the University of Nairobi that I learned about God's plan of salvation. It was there I accepted Jesus as my personal Savior. Precisely sixteen years after my father's words, "Muli, you will repeat Standard Seven," my schooling culminated with a Ph.D. from the University of Wyoming.

Through my experiences, I have learned several lessons. Always take positive steps of faith in the circumstances that God brings into your life. Always turn to God *first* in any situation, not as a last choice. Accept failures as stepping stones. Never allow other people's failures to be a stumbling block. Always see yourself for what you can be in the future, not necessarily based on what you are now. And *never give up!*

Dr. Vincent Muli Wa Kituku, author, columnist and adjunct professor, has dedicated his life to nurturing the human spirit. A native of Kenya, he earned a Ph.D. from the University of Wyoming in 1991. Dr. Kituku is an award-winning speaker/storyteller who motivates his audiences to identify and effectively face their "spiritual and social buffaloes."

Web site: www.kituku.com
Phone: 1-888- 685-1621.

## "I Am No Longer Your Competition"

### Donna Hatasaki

Gangsters and their girlfriends packed the East Palo Alto theater. Police officers formed a fence along the walls. The fourth-largest drug dealer in that west coast city stood center stage to make an announcement. The air was thick, saturated with tension like an odorless gas that might instantly explode. The twenty-four-year-old man at center stage thrust his business beeper into the air and declared before an audience of his fellow drug lords: "I am no longer your competition."

No gangsters stormed the stage that day. No police moved to make an arrest. There was no flash fire in the theater, only the beginning of a slow burn, a burn that moved across the landscape of Juan Ibarra's life for the next two years, slowly consuming every thing and every person in its path.

Juan recommitted his life to Jesus Christ that evening, following a hard-core outreach play reflecting a life much like his own. The decision sparked a "fire" that cleared from his life at least six years of thorns and tangled thickets that were choking out any growth from his first decision to follow Jesus as a sophomore in high school.

He had come to Young Life as a fledgling drug dealer his freshman year of high school and became instantly addicted to the atmosphere of fun.

"I couldn't stop going to club. All week I'd sell drugs, get in fights, do everything. But on club day I'd quit," he says.

Juan forged his parents' signature on the camp forms the summer after his sophomore year and spent a life-changing week at Woodleaf, the Young Life camp in Northern California. He spent the next few years following Christ as best he could, but by the time he turned nineteen he had chosen a different path—one that led him often to San Francisco to pick up cocaine.

But that path perished in the theater "fire" and Juan was ready to consider the call to Young Life ministry. In 1991 he made the move to Young Life staff.

Juan lost his family as a result of the "fire" from the theater—the "family" he had constructed from a dozen desperate young men, the family known on the street as The Mob.

"I've been asked, 'What was the hardest thing for you to lose? The money?' No. To have the people who were like my family spit on me, call me a traitor, a coward—that was the hardest thing for me to face."

But losing the money wasn't easy either. For two years he watched his treasures turn to ashes— his designer suits, his nice home, his fleet of ten cars including the Saab, the BMW, the customized '65 Mustang. Without a $15,000 a week income from drug sales, he couldn't make his payments. Finally Juan found himself living in one room of his father-in-law's home with his wife and three children. And he found himself depressed.

"I couldn't even afford to buy my kids diapers. I said, 'What kind of man am I?' "

One day an old friend called Juan out of genuine concern. He offered a $20,000 drug deal— easy in, easy out. A quick answer to Juan's problems. A tempting ointment for his ego, scorched as it was.

"I was trembling," he recalls. "I wanted to take the deal. Finally I said, 'If you're really my friend, don't ever ask me that again. I can't trade my salvation for $20,000.' "

Nothing was left of Juan except a desire to follow Jesus. But that was all he needed the day Clif Davidson asked him to consider a call to Young Life staff. Clif, Regional Director for the San Francisco Bay Region, had been searching East Palo Alto for an indigenous leader for some time. Juan Ibarra seemed the perfect person for the job.

At center stage in the theater, Juan had declared to the drug lords that he was no longer their competition. He meant what he said, but what he said was untrue. As a member of the Young Life staff, Juan was the worst kind of competition for every drug dealer in East Palo Alto. He was undermining their market by providing a different addiction for the kids.

"Instead of recruiting kids and showing them how to use guns, I was showing them how to read the Bible. Instead of making plans with them for stealing and doing violence, I was giving them plans for the kingdom."

Today Juan is claiming a significant segment of the drug dealers' clientele. Each week more than eighty kids walk into the Young Life house where Juan and his wife Sofima live with their four kids. On Thursday afternoons, for example, as many as forty kids pile out of the school bus down the block and make their way to Juan and Sofima's for the evening.

The first hour of "club" on Thursday is an hour set aside for homework.

"You can't play until you've shown me your work," Juan reminds the middle school kids who are already busy with their books. By four o'clock the books are closed and the balls are bouncing. Basketballs, fooseballs, Ping-Pong™balls. It's free play until Juan bellows out across the crowd, "OK, everybody against the wall."

The kids don't question his authority: they move readily into position. He has earned a respect they don't pay to many people—credibility that comes from caring for the kids day in and day out. It's easy to imagine Juan on a street corner calling out orders to his gang. It's moving to recognize the redemption of his gifts.

Juan walks the wall with a camera, ordering kids to make the craziest face they can muster for a contest that undoubtedly will end with everyone winning a prize. Kids you might steer clear of if you met them on the street stretch their cheeks, bug their eyes, stick out their tongues and pose. It's a moment of sheer foolishness in the midst of an otherwise oppressive week.

Three or four foolish skits later, Juan calls the now rowdy roomful of kids back to attention against the wall. It's time to talk about Jesus. They listen with respect.

After the talk it's time to eat. Outside, a volunteer has been busy grilling burgers; for some kids it is the only home-cooked meal they will eat until next week.

Juan ends the evening with a reminder that an improved report card means a prize at Young Life. Kids devour his concern like the burgers from the grill. For some his words are the only encouragement they will hear until next week. It's no wonder the kids beg Juan to add extra evenings of club. They are addicted to the atmosphere of fun. They are hooked on the hope of love and kindness.

Drug dealers beware. Your competition is back. He's been through a fire, but now business is better than it was before the blaze.

Adapted from an article by the same title from the April/May 1997 issue of *Relationships*, a publication of Young Life. Used by permission.

Juan Ibarra

Donna Hatasaki is Assistant to the President of Young Life, a ministry to reach adolescents for Christ in this country and around the world. She has written for several publications, including *The Journey Begins*, a journal for helping teenagers begin the life-long journey of following Jesus (available through the Young Life International Service Center, Colorado Springs, CO). She has been a volunteer leader with Young Life for sixteen years and lives in Mountain View, CA, with her husband, Grant, and two children, Joseph and Allison.

Address: 119 Concord Circle, Mountain View, CA, 94040
E-mail: dhatasaki @sc.younglife.org.

## To Mrs. Russell

## *Jason Wrench*

Growing up, I was the child everyone dreaded to have show up in his classroom. I was unruly, talkative and slow. As early as kindergarten the teachers decided I was too slow to keep up with the other children, so I was placed with other slow learners.

Throughout my elementary career I was anything but the ideal pupil. I was a troublemaker. In the second grade, pupils who misbehaved were forced to wear a red block of wood with a gigantic sad face painted on it. A pupil wearing the block could talk to no one but the teacher. I think I still have a rope chafe from where the rope holding the block bit into the back of my neck almost daily.

My grades were poor. If I was lucky, I got the occasional C. The best my parents hoped for was that one day I would actually be allowed to graduate high school, or at least get a GED and go to work at some fast-food restaurant.

In the third grade, my teacher truly disliked me. After my grandfather visited one day, he demanded that I be removed from the teacher's classroom because of the spiteful and mean-spirited way she related to me.

When I was in the fourth grade, the "resource" classroom (a euphemistic term used for a classroom of slower pupils) was taken away because the school needed the space for "normal" pupils. After searching throughout the entire building, the administration decided that our class was to be held in a janitor's storeroom.

Throughout my entire elementary career I was constantly being told by teachers and administrators that I was stupid, slow and just not good enough to be with the other pupils. To say that my self-esteem was shot would be putting it nicely. I felt dumb, bad and useless. I felt that God had made a mistake.

Being forced to wear the red "sad-face" block symbolized that *I* had made a mistake; and it caused me to become introverted and unaware of life's joys. Being told I wasn't good enough to have a classroom, but that there was a lovely janitor's storeroom where I could learn made me think that I was only as good as the trash that inhabited my classroom. Constantly being told that there was no hope for me and that I might as well not even try had killed the spirit of a once bright and eager child.

At the beginning of my sixth grade year, I was given the opportunity to join the school orchestra. The only problem was that if I joined the orchestra I would not be able to be in "resource" any longer. My parents and the school administrators hashed it out and I was allowed to join the orchestra. I joined the mainstream of the school for the first time.

My homeroom teacher that year was a gentle woman of about forty-five. She welcomed me into her class on the first day of school with a big smile.

The sixth graders were located in portable classrooms the school district used in overload situations. Before this, all of my classes had been in what they called "open concept" classrooms—no walls or doors between connecting classrooms. In these classrooms, students could see and hear everything going on in the classes around them. This always made it extremely hard for me to focus; and since I was a poor student anyway, I had always been placed in the back of the room near the other classrooms. For the first time now, I was in a classroom where I could see and hear only *my* teacher and focus on what *she* was saying, without all the distractions that previously had been around me.

My homeroom teacher was Mrs. Russell. She was a first-year teacher at my school, though she had been teaching for years elsewhere. She was friendly and had a genuine desire to teach. She was negative only when she had to discipline a child.

Mrs. Russell decided at the beginning of the year that every student in the room was to have a specific job within the classroom. I was quickly assigned to be the desk monitor. I think I got this particular job because my desk was the most horrendous mess anyone could ever imagine.

My job was simple. After school each day I would check everyone's desk and make sure it was clean. If it was, I would put a blue piece of paper on it. A pupil collecting five blue strips would get candy from Mrs. Russell. If the desk was dirty, the pupil would receive a yellow strip of paper and be forced to give up all blue strips. A pupil receiving two yellows would be held after school in detention.

Actually, I was the one who came up with the entire idea. Mrs. Russell continued to use this system for checking desks until the day she retired in May 1997.

For the first time in my life I had a passion about something. I loved the power that being desk monitor gave me. I never once abused the power because I knew that Mrs. Russell had instilled trust in me to be just and fair. Over and over she would compliment me on doing a great job.

She also would say things like, "You're going to grow up and be something pretty special." Or, "You can do anything you want in life, Jason, as long as you put your mind to it."

Mrs. Russell was the first teacher who had ever been nice to me. She showed me that I was a person—a good person, despite what the "sad face" block had said. She told me that I was smart; I just had to apply myself and do the work. She taught me that I was worthy of living as a human being. Many people talk about the one teacher who changed their lives; mine would definitely be Mrs. Russell.

That year my grades went from C's and D's to A's and B's. This dramatic change came simply because one teacher loved and cared enough to take the time to work with me and show me how much she cared. As a wise person once said about school children, "They don't care how much you know until they know how much you care!"

At the end of my sixth grade year Mrs. Russell encouraged me to apply to the honors junior high school. I discussed it with my parents and we decided that I should try to apply. I filled out the paperwork and acquired the proper recommendations, but figured I had no chance of making it.

About a month later, my principal announced over the loudspeaker that anyone who had applied to a magnet school needed to come to the main office. All of the students who had applied to the honors junior high milled around the room. Some leered at me, wondering what the "dummy" was doing there.

Since my last name starts with a "W," I was the last one to get the letter of acceptance or rejection. I took a huge breath and gulped as I slowly read the letter. *I was in!*

I leaped for joy and told everyone I saw. I had gone from being one of the dumb "resource" kids to being in an honors junior high school. A number of students who had previously stuck their noses in the air when I walked by, thinking of me as the "dummy," didn't make it into the school. I had finally come around in my academic life. Not only did I go to the honors junior high, but I also went to the honors high school.

My road to academic and intellectual maturity has been a tough one. I often wonder how many kids like myself are left on the side of the academic road, how many never meet their Mrs. Russell and therefore never achieve their potential. I also wonder where I would be if I had not had a teacher who showed me she cared.

Currently I am working on my master's degree. I also teach public speaking at the university level. Mrs. Russell has inspired me to be the kind of teacher she was for me. I hope I will always recognize a diamond in the rough. I hope I will never ignore a student, thinking that he or she is just not smart enough. I hope I will boost students' self-esteem, not destroy it. Mrs. Russell is a very hard act to follow as a teacher, but is a wonderful role model.

I'll never forget the day I went back to my old elementary school for Mrs. Russell's retirement party. I hadn't stepped foot in that building since I left. I had kept in touch with Mrs. Russell, though. When I graduated from high school, she and her husband sent me a graduation present. When I had a brief stint as a radio talk show host for a Christian radio station, Mrs. Russell was my biggest fan.

Walking into that school brought a flood of emotions upon me. I looked at the door that led to the janitor's closet where I had spent much of the fourth grade. I saw the old classrooms and felt the torment that went along with those rooms. But then there was Mrs. Russell, the woman to whom I had come to say "Thank you." Even now as I write, I still have huge tears swell in my eyes as I think about her generosity and loving spirit.

I gave her a small teddy bear (the school's mascot) with a huge bouquet of balloons from my family. (My dad had wanted to build a monument in her honor, but that would have been going a little overboard, right?) I also gave her a copy of a paper I had written about her in college which dealt with an event or person who changed your life.

It often amazes me how God knows when we need someone the most, and miraculously places them in our lives at those times. Without Mrs. Russell in my life, who knows where I would have gone and what I would have done?

When I got my undergraduate degree, I dedicated my thesis (just as I will for my master's thesis and my doctoral dissertation) to "Mrs. Russell—Without you this never would have happened."

Jason Wrench is President of Road Speakers International, his self-initiated speaking and writing firm. He received training from Florence Littauer and is now a Certified Personality Plus Trainer. He is currently working on his Master's degree at Texas Tech University in Lubbock, Texas, and plans to pursue a doctoral program.

Web site: http://www.members.aol.com/ttujay/page
E-mail: TTUJAY@ aol.com

## A New Perspective

### Joni Eareckson Tada

*Editor's Note:* On a hot July afternoon, seventeen-year-old Joni Eareckson dove into the cool water of Chesapeake Bay. In the next instant her entire life was transformed from that of an active young woman to that of a quadriplegic who would spend the rest of her life in a wheelchair. From that tragic beginning has emerged one of the most remarkable bounce back stories of our time, as Joni struggled to accept her disability and discover the spiritual meaning of her life.

It was summer, 1969, two years after my diving accident. I thought of the many things which had happened to me during those two incredible years. In taking inventory of my spiritual life, I found it consisted mainly of fantastic highs and lows—but mostly lows. In fact, I'd recently climbed out of the worst depression I'd experienced since the accident. If I didn't receive some help, some mature guidance, I knew I'd sink again. It was only a matter of time.

I made as much progress in rehabilitation as was physically possible. It was evident now I'd never walk again; I'd never get the use of my hands again; I'd forever be paralyzed from the neck down, unable to even care for my own personal needs. It was certain now that I'd be forever dependent on others for every physical comfort or function.

This dependency was enough, in itself, to trigger another bout with depression and self-pity, and I talked about my concerns with Diana. [Diana White, a friend from high school days and a fellow member of Young Life, a Christian youth ministry]

"I have this tremendous feeling of hopelessness and worthlessness, Di," I told her. "I'm praying that the Lord will do something in my life to show me that it has meaning."

"I've been praying, too, Joni," she replied, adding, "you know, I'm going to bring a friend over to meet you."

"Who? Why?"

"Steve Estes. You don't know him, but he's at just the opposite side of things spiritually. He has a love for the Lord and knowledge of the Scriptures that really ought to help."

"Sure," I volunteered without much enthusiasm.

"He's a young guy. In fact, he's still in high school."

"High school?! Diana! He's a kid?"

"No—don't judge. Wait 'til you meet him."

Steve Estes came over to the house that evening, and the minute he walked through the door, he shattered all my preconceived notions about him.

Steve loomed tall above my wheelchair and his piercing green eyes immediately communicated an attitude of warmth and openness. In the introductory conversation which followed, he made me completely at ease. He evidenced maturity and comfortable self-assurance, and one of the first things I noticed was his attitude toward me.

Many people who meet me for the first time seem awkward and uncomfortable with the chair. It intimidates them or causes them to pity me. It usually takes several visits and conversations for us to move past the chair and deal on an ordinary level. Unfortunately, some people never get to that point, and consequently, I usually feel self-conscious.

Yet Steve was completely at ease, making me comfortable too. He talked fast, expressing himself with animated gestures, and seemed enthusiastic about everything. As we conversed, he began to share biblical concepts—ideas that were exciting to him and stimulating to me.

"Joni," he said earnestly, "isn't it great what God is doing in different people's lives today?"

*What? Who? Where?* I was too embarrassed to ask the questions as they popped in my mind. It didn't matter. Steve answered them for me.

"Kids are experiencing fantastic things in Young Life at Woodlawn. And in our church, we've seen God's Spirit make a lot of people really come alive. One couple was on the verge of divorce—God brought 'em back together. One guy was heavy into dope and Christ saved him. A girl I know was really messed up inside, and the Lord straightened her out. Man, you should see her today!"

The stories came rapid-fire, and I began to see a new reality to God's power. The Lord had worked in people's lives and the truth and meaning of it spilled over into Steve's experience and then into mine through Steve's recounting.

Steve himself had seen God demonstrate His love and power. Steve's faith, energy and spiritual maturity were evidently the qualities that made him so different from me. He radiated trust, love for Christ and self-assured success. It was amazing to me that a sixteen-year-old could offer so much spiritual insight and wisdom. As a young adult of twenty, I had not come as far. There was something about him, a quality in his life, that I wanted. He radiated confidence, poise and authority. He spoke convincingly of the Lord and the simple, quiet strength that faith in Christ brings to a life.

"Steve, what you say is like fresh new truth," I said to him excitedly. "Please come back and tell me more."

"Sure, I'd like that."

"Can you help me get what you have? I'm a Christian, but there's so much I don't know about the Lord. You have so much more spiritual knowledge than I do."

"Joni, what would you say if I came over every Wednesday and had a Bible study with you?" he suggested.

"Great," I answered.

Diana was smiling and nodding. "I'm going to be there too and maybe Jay [Joni's sister] and others would like to come. Is that all right?"

"Sure," Steve smiled. It was strange. Here was a boy, just sixteen, planning to teach a group of young adults about the Christian faith. Yet no one questioned his authority or ability to do so. Even then he had the eloquence and charisma of a spiritual teacher, a minister. Everyone respected him and responded to his qualities of leadership.

Steve enjoyed the challenge. He said, "Joni, your house really makes me feel comfortable. It's like a retreat—the atmosphere makes me feel like we're at *L'Abri* with Francis Schaeffer."

He sensed that I—and some of the others—had not really mastered some of the basic Christian doctrines—the character of God, deity of Christ, sin, repentance and salvation—and these became the focus of our weekly Bible studies.

"In Ephesians," he explained, "Paul tells us that we have a fantastic heritage: Christ *chose us* even before He made the world. He created us, in His image, for a particular purpose. God wants us to grow and excel, to be successful. A lot of people are confused about what true spirituality is. If a guy knows a lot of Bible verses, he's often thought of as spiritual. But having head knowledge of Bible truth isn't spirituality. True spirituality is putting God's Word into practice—making His truth valid by actually doing what He says and not just pointing to it as a nice standard."

As Steve shared basic Bible doctrine with us, I began to see the shallowness of my own faith and spirituality. My spiritual ups and downs could be charted as easily and accurately as my physical progress. This became something I wanted to overcome, something I wanted to deal with in a positive way. I began to look to the spiritual principles and revolve my life around them for a change.

Alone with God, I recalled how I'd withdrawn from reality and turned my back on Him so often. I confessed, "Lord, I've been wrong—wrong to try and shut You out. Forgive me, God. Thank You for this new understanding of Your Word which Steve has shared. Please forgive me and bring me back to You—back into fellowship with You once more." The Holy Spirit began to convict, then teach me. With each succeeding week, spiritual truth became more real, and I began to see life from God's perspective.

I learned that God's Word is a handbook for sensible living; He doesn't give us instructions without reason.

I saw, in fact, that God tries to warn us in Scripture; for example, sex before marriage is wrong.

There seem to be so many more warnings in the Bible about illicit sex as compared to warnings about other sinful conduct or behavior, such as gossip, envy, lying and anger. The Bible says of these, "Resist the devil" (James 4:7)—stand and fight and overcome these faults. But as for sexual sin and sensuality, the Bible says, "flee" (1 Corinthians 6:18). If I had been obedient and not given in to temptations, I would not have been tormented by longings and desires which now could never be satisfied. They were like an unquenched thirst. No matter how much I shut out reality and lived the experiences in fantasy, it could never be the same. The feelings were shadow substance and unsatisfying.

I had learned some painful lessons from my relationship with Jason [a high school boyfriend]. Now I reaped the consequences. I was tortured, but not because I had done something ugly and repulsive. On the contrary, physical love is beautiful and exciting. Yet God knows how it frustrates and torments without the context of marriage. I was lusting after memories. I know other girls who have cried bitter tears over the same thing. They have found that guilt and remorse over sex outside of marriage can cloud and ruin otherwise happy lives and handicap otherwise successful marriages.

But now, with God's help and forgiveness, I repented and put all that behind me. I prayed for His direction and the mental willpower to think His thoughts and not wallow in self-pity and lustful memories and fantasies.

I concentrated on the fact that, once and for all, I had to forget the past and concentrate on the present, trusting God, claiming the promise of Scripture that God separates our sins from us forever (Psalm 103:12).

I decided to rid myself of as many reminders of the past as I could. I gave away my cherished hockey and lacrosse sticks, sold my horse, Tumbleweed, and got rid of all the other *things* that tied me to the old memories.

Now I was forced to trust God. I had no alternative but to thank Him for what He was going to do with my future.

As I began to pray and depend on Him, He did not disappoint me. Before, I'd say, "Lord, I want to do Your will—and Your will is for me to get back on my feet or, at least, get my hands back." I was deciding His will for me and rebelling when things didn't turn out as I planned.

Now I wept for all those lost months filled with bitterness and sinful attitudes. I prayed for an understanding of His will for my life. What was God's will for my life? To find out, I had to believe that all that had happened to me was an important part of that plan. I read, "In every thing give thanks: for this is the will of God in Christ Jesus concerning you" (1 Thessalonians

5:18, KJV). God's will was for me to be thankful in everything? OK. I blindly trusted that this was truth. I thanked God for what He did and what He was going to do.

As I concentrated on His positive instruction from the Bible, it was no longer necessary to retreat from reality. Feelings no longer seemed important. Fantasies of having physical feeling and touch were no longer necessary because I learned that I was only temporarily deprived of these sensations. The Bible indicates that our bodies are temporal. Therefore, my paralysis was temporal. When my focus shifted to this eternal perspective, all my concerns about being in a wheelchair became trivial.

Steve continued to come, sometimes several times a week. His Bible-based teaching of simple doctrinal truth was becoming a part of my life. Before, I had accepted doctrine pretty much without question. But it was not real in my experience. Its truth had not been tested. In my earlier depression, I had examined other philosophical and theological points of view. It was no longer possible for me to accept doctrine without question, but even as I questioned, answers were provided. Steve explained Bible truth in such a way that it was as if the Lord spoke directly to me.

I saw Steve's coming into my life as a specific answer to the desperate prayer I had prayed just before I met him.

We discussed the second coming of Jesus Christ. I learned that one day Jesus would return to earth and I'd get a brand-new body. Christ would give me a glorified body that could do everything I could do before—probably even more. Some day I would have feeling again! *I won't be paralyzed forever.*

This new perspective made it unnecessary for me to retreat into fantasy trips or daydreams anymore.

Steve helped me end my cycle of peaks and valleys of spiritual progress. "Set your minds on things above," he read from Colossians 3:2, "not on earthly things." Since I could see that one day I'd have a renewed body, it became easy for me to focus my desires on heavenly, eternal things. I had already lost temporal things—the use of my earthly body—so it was easy to accept this truth. Although "condemned" to a wheelchair, I knew one day I'd be free of it.

"Steve," I said to him, "I'm beginning to see the chair more as a tool than a tragedy. I believe God is going to teach me something more about this!"

Steve introduced me to the process of putting God's Word into practice, of acting on His promises and commands. I would read something in the Bible and consciously say, "This is God's will." Intellectually, I understood the meaning of it. Emotionally, I had to put this new truth to the test, to prove it by my own will. "Yes, this is God's will," adding, "for me."

"Lord, I'm trusting You to bring me through all this victoriously," I reminded Him. Scripture took on personal meaning. Job had suffered, so he could speak convincingly to my needs. Jeremiah had suffered, and I learned from him, too. Since Paul had endured beatings, shipwrecks, imprisonment and ill health, I related to his sufferings as well. I began to see what the Bible calls a "fellowship of suffering."

I memorized Scripture portions that had great meaning to me. Understanding these passages that spoke to my needs enabled me to better trust God with my will as well as my life. Even when distressing or despondent times came along, I could depend on the fact that "He knows what He is doing," as Daddy frequently said.

Through memorizing God's promises, I learned that the Lord would take me out of training in this school of suffering—but in His own good time. The apostle Paul wrote that the key was to keep forever striving. Even he, at the peak of his life and commitment to Christ, admitted that he had not arrived spiritually.

*Probably,* I thought, *my suffering and training are a lifelong process. It will end only when I go to be with Christ.*

There was a lot of catching up for me to do. If life was going to mean anything, I'd have to learn everything I could—not just spiritual truth, but academic understanding as well. I'd have to find a way to make some kind of contribution to society.

I began to understand spiritual truth in meaningful ways. This new understanding gave me victory over past sin, temptation and depression. God had given me the means to control my sinful nature when I realized the importance of His reality and the present.

The fantasies ended. Forever. With God's complete fulfillment. I didn't need to relive memories from the past. I had come to the place where my body no longer needed the sensations I once thought so terribly important. God had taken me beyond the need for feeling and touching. Yet, He saw to it that, whenever possible, I could enjoy such things as the feel of a cashmere sweater on my cheek, a hug from someone I care about, the reassuring movement of a rocking chair and the sensations He brought every time I went outside—wind, sun, even rain on my face. And I was grateful for all He gave.

From *Joni* by Joni Eareckson Tada, © 1996 Joni Eareckson Tada and Joe Musser. Zondervan Publishing House, Grand Rapids, MI. Used by permission.

 Joni Eareckson Tada is founder and president of JAF Ministries (Joni and Friends), an organization accelerating Christian outreach in the disability community. Joni is the author of twenty-two books, including her autobiography, *Joni,* which has also been made into a full-length feature film now shown in scores of languages in countries around the world. She is a successful artist, writer and speaker and serves on several boards for organizations

which benefit the disabled. Joni has received numerous honors and awards from colleges and universities for her humanitarian work, most recently an honorary doctorate in Humane Letters from Columbia University in 1998. Joni and her husband, Ken, have been married for sixteen years.

## Section 2

## Straight from the Teens

*You will seek me and find me when
you seek me with all your heart.*
(Jeremiah 29:13)

The young people whose stories appear in this
section either are now in their teen years or have
only recently left those years behind. Every story
here, whether written in the first person or told
by someone close to them, reflects moments of
heartache, soul-searching and progress toward
victory.

Life will continue to present challenges, temptations—perhaps even suffering—to those young
Christians whose stories are written here. They
will go through testing times as well as the high
times of joy—don't we all? In James we read,
"Count it all joy . . . when you meet various trials,
for you know the testing of your faith produces
steadfastness" (1:2-3, RSV). Because they have
learned to take *everything* to the Lord, I believe
they will continue to triumph over adversity as
they rely on *His* promises and *His* strength. They
will be winners.

# Getting High on God

## Joseph J. Ortega

Twice I went on a trip and came back a different person. The first time was when I was thirteen. It was 1996, the summer after I finished eighth grade. My parents had been split up since I was three years old. Every summer and a couple of Christmases I would go down from Boise, Idaho and visit my dad in Arizona. We had been really close when I was little, but later I got resentful toward him because I believed my dad had hurt my mom by leaving.

I went to Arizona that summer as a straight-A student with a good outlook on life. When I came back, I wasn't the same.

There was a lot of strife while I was there because of little things I said. I know that much of what happened there was my fault.

At the time, my dad had two young sons and when I got there I could see that he and I weren't as close as we had been before. He didn't pay much attention to me. He just played with his two little boys. Like any teenager, I was jealous. I took it out on my little brothers. I was mean to them, and my dad didn't like that. We got into fights every single day, and it got to the point where he finally kicked me out.

It ended up in a lot of pain. I came back to Boise really changed. When I got back I told my mom, "Don't touch me. Don't talk to me."

I had been a good kid before—a really sweet kid, but now I was depressed and full of hatred and resentment. Perfect timing for the devil to get hold of my life! When I was feeling so low and looking for ways to make myself happier, the devil moved right in.

When I went back to school, my grades went down to all D's. That's when the devil sent some people my way that weren't right for me. They offered me a way to find "happiness." By then, I thought the only way I could find happiness was in drugs.

I started out slow, just hanging out with some druggie kids. After a while I started doing it. I started with pot, and then that wasn't enough so I moved on to doing crack and crank and then speed. Finally, I started doing heroin. My motto was: Get up. Get high. Get drunk. Have fun.

At that time I couldn't stand my parents. I hated my life, and even tried suicide a few times.

At first my mom didn't realize I was using drugs. The only person in my family who knew I was doing drugs was my second-oldest sister,

Sabrina. My mom knew that if I were to confide in anybody, it would be Sabrina.

One day I was going out and my mom asked me where I was going. I told her it was none of her business and I'd be back when I wanted to come back. My mom said, "You know, Joey, I talked to Sabrina and I know you're doing drugs."

I was really mad. I said, "I can't believe she told you!"

Actually, Sabrina hadn't said anything to my mom, but saying that was the only way she could find out for sure if I was using drugs.

The next turning point in my life came when I went on another trip—this time an unexpected one. One day in April when I was at school, I got this message in my classroom: "Emergency! Be out in front of the school immediately." I thought, *Oh my gosh, something's happened.* I went outside and all of a sudden, my mom's car came screeching around the corner. I got into the car and kept asking, "What's going on? What's happening?"

My mom wouldn't say anything. She had taken all she could take of my verbal abuse. I looked in the back of the car and saw toothpaste and clothes and stuff. I said, "What's this? Are we going on vacation?"

No answer.

Then I realized that everything in the backseat was mine. "Are you trying to get rid of me?" I yelled.

All she would say was, "Shut up, Joey. Just shut up!"

What had happened, I later learned, was that she had heard about a weekend Christian convention for teens called "Acquire the Fire." It was going to be held in Denver, Colorado and she had heard about it just that day—the day the local youth group was leaving.

She had called the coordinator and asked, "Is there any way my son can go along on this trip?"

He said, "No, the bus is full."

At that, my mom was really downhearted, but she started praying. About two hours later, the coordinator called and said, "One of the other kids can't make it, so we do have one spot on the bus." Mom quickly packed my bags and called the school (which explained the "emergency" call).

She drove like crazy. She had less than one hour to pay the money, go home and get all my stuff packed, pick me up and drive back downtown. Finally we pulled up by a church where a van loaded with kids was about to leave. Mom practically threw me into the van, then got back in her car and didn't even look at me. She just drove off.

I just sat there in the van with a bunch of church kids. Even though I was rebellious and for sure didn't know why I had been thrown in with this bunch, I knew it was a church thing so I didn't swear or anything like that. In fact, I didn't talk to anyone. People would talk to me and I just sat there and didn't say anything.

We got to Twin Falls, pulled up at a big church, got in a Greyhound bus and started out for Colorado. Well, this is where God came in. It was only supposed to be a sixteen-hour drive to Denver, but it ended up being a twenty-eight hour drive. Our bus broke down four times. I was in the back listening to my radio with my head down so I could ignore the other people. But every time the bus broke down, we had to get out and group up, and I was forced to talk to the other people.

Just talking to them began to soften my heart. God was opening me up to other people. It was like God was saying "You're not going to get down to Denver until you start talking."

Finally, we got to Denver and I went to the Teen Convention "Acquire the Fire," which was put on by Teen Mania Ministries. This group puts on about twenty-eight conventions around the country each year. They have giant video screens, pyrotechnics and popular Christian rock groups like "Jars of Clay" and "Newsboys."

The first night of the convention, I kind of kept a closed mind. I had been raised in a Christian family, but I was thinking, *Hey, I tried this stuff and it didn't work for me.* So I just sat there and tuned out.

Then this guy who was an ex-gangster came up to speak. His life had been just like mine. He told about how he got into drugs, alcohol and gangs. He said, "I thought I loved being high, but now I love being high on God."

The next day I thought about everything he had said. I went back on Saturday, and the ending session was so powerful I just started bawling. I said, "God, give me one more try. Please help me. I need *something*."

That day I gave my life to God, and from then on I had no craving for cigarettes, alcohol or drugs—not at all. I have had no desire for them at all from that day on. I didn't need them anymore. I knew it had to be God.

When I got home, I went in and gave my mom a big hug.

When I went back to school, all my friends kept saying, "Why don't you come back to our house and we'll show what you've been missing, 'cause you're really goin' off the high wall here."

I just said, "No, I'm stopping now, you guys." In fact, I actually led two of them to Christ. I don't know where they are now, but I pray for them.

Things are still tense with my dad, but I'm working on that, and I've built a close relationship with my mom and stepfather, and an even closer one with God.

I start each day with an hour of quiet time when I study and meditate on Scripture. God is in my life every day. He gives me what I need to get through even the toughest trials.

When I was at the convention in Colorado, they would take us one-by-one and talk to us about what it means to give your heart to Christ. It sunk in. When I got back I was doing really well, but my mom worried that the spiritual high would gradually begin to wear off—especially over the summer months.

My mom called Teen Mania to ask about summer missions. They send about 3,000 teens on missions around the world each summer. She signed me up to go on a mission to Panama for the summer. She didn't really have the money for it, but an unexpected bonus at work gave her the deposit and I was able to raise the rest of the cost through sponsorships from family and friends.

First, we had intensive drama training for about a week in Florida. The dramas are twenty-four-minute pantomimes to recorded music. You have to be exactly on the beats—you find yourself counting the beats even in your sleep at night. They give you parts for each pantomime. After each drama the leader would explain the meaning of the play and the importance of salvation to our audience. One play we performed, called *The Journeyman*, depicts people's everyday lives, with Jesus coming in between each scene saying, "Come to Me." It has a powerful ending where Jesus is crucified and resurrected.

One time we hiked and canoed deep into the jungle to a village where the natives had never seen white people before. Some of the people came to Christ. It was hard work, but I look back and think, *Look at the reward*.

The next summer (1997) I went on a mission trip to Africa. I enjoyed this trip even more than the first one. Most of us in the group were strong Christians on a rampage to go save souls for Christ. We had a play called *Allegiance* where I played the part of Jesus.

When I went back to school after the trip to Africa, I really missed my Christian friends. I actually cried. But I stay in contact with them and we keep each other pumped up and on track. My time in Panama and Africa deepened my appreciation for every little thing that comes into my life.

I thank God for turning my life around, and now I'm permanently "high on God."

 Joseph ("Joey") Ortega lives in Meridian, Idaho, just outside of Boise, and is a 1999 graduate of Eagle High School. He spent the summers of 1996 and 1997 doing missionary work in foreign countries with Teen Mania, a Christian organization that sends about 3,000 teens on missions around the world each summer. Joey plans to go to India on his next missionary trip, and then to work as an intern at Teen Mania's "Acquire the Fire" conventions held in various locations around the country.

## Lost and Alone

## Monica Johnson

I was seventeen and all alone, sitting on a hill in Santa Cruz, California, overlooking the bay. Everything around me was still except for the waves rolling in and crashing on the sand below. My heart was aching, and tears trickled down my face. I lay my head in my hands and asked myself, *How did my life get so out of control?*

I sat there crying and then, without thinking, looked up into the clear, starry sky and words just flowed from me: "God, please give me back my life, or else please take me home to You. I can't go on like this!" I kept talking to the sky—to God—until finally I fell asleep on the hill.

My story is not an uncommon one, but for me it was unique and devastating. From the age of eight until I was fourteen, I was living a nightmare from which I couldn't wake up. I was being abused by the man I called "Dad." He said he

117

was teaching me how a man and a woman love each other. As the years went by I got wise to what was going on, so he got me hooked on a drug called "speed." This drug made me numb, so the abuse seemed like a dream while it was happening.

At night I would cry myself to sleep, asking God why this was happening to me. As I got older, my sense of self-worth went down the drain. Every night I would ask God to make it stop—to make this man go away and leave me alone. But as time went on I came to believe God wasn't listening and didn't care.

Finally, an anonymous person turned my stepfather in for child molestation and he was arrested and put in prison. My sister and I were placed in a group home, then later were sent to my aunt and uncle's home.

Things were hard for everyone around me. I was fourteen and on drugs, and the Lord was completely blocked from my heart. The drugs had me totally confused. I ended up in a rehab center for a year. I completed the rehab program and returned to high school and my aunt and uncle's home.

It was a new start, but somehow I never felt quite right. It wasn't long before I relapsed and ran away. That's when I ended up praying and sleeping on the top of that hill in Santa Cruz.

The next morning I called my friend, Zak, who took me to an alcoholic recovery program meeting that night. Zak also introduced me to a friend of his who was willing to put me up in a motel room for a while. I was young, foolish and appreciative of the kindness. Not long after that I found out I was going to be a mother.

Everything began to change for me after that night of earnest prayer on the hill overlooking the bay. It didn't happen all at once, but I know that was the turning point. That was seven years ago.

When my daughter, Christina, was born, I discovered the miracle of love. I suddenly wanted to live—for my daughter and for myself. For the very first time I had a reason to love and a reason to live.

Five years ago, I met Glen and his little son, Daniel. Soon we became a family. I believe the Lord brought us together to raise our two children together. Now we have four wonderful kids. Glen and I have another son and daughter together. Glen loves my daughter, Christina, the same as he loves his own children. I feel the same way about Daniel. We are a happy family.

We feel very at home in our church. Christina and I were baptized in the Boise River in the summer of 1998. The rest of our family goes to church with us, and I'm sure they will soon be baptized, too. My favorite scripture is Ephesians 2:8 which says, "For it is by grace you have been saved, through faith—and this not from yourselves, it is the gift of God."

The Lord blessed me seven years ago with the strength to go on. Now my life is truly blessed each day with my wonderful family, and most of all with Jesus in my heart. I look back now and realize God was always there with me. I just couldn't see Him because I was in pain and on drugs. I know the Holy Spirit was there for me because I am still here today, and I'm clean and sober.

I thank the Lord every day for the spiritual high I have found in Him. All those years ago, I didn't have a plan or even think of the future—I just wanted out. Now the Lord's plan for my life is shining through and His plan is awesome. Praise the Lord!

Monica Johnson is a homemaker and mother of four. She has a supportive husband, and lives in Boise, Idaho. In July of 1998 she and her seven-year-old daughter were baptized in the Boise River by the pastor of their church. Monica worked as a teen counselor when she was a teen herself. She has a dream of becoming a counselor for abused children. She is now working part-time with AmeriCorps in a children/parent literacy program. She enjoys writing, exercising to music and being a mom. Monica hopes her story will inspire or help some young person to find faith again.

# To Tell or Not to Tell

## MacKenzie Bennett

A sudden cold feeling of shock came over me even though it was a warm summer afternoon.

I was twelve that summer. We had moved to this community about six months earlier when my dad was called to be the pastor of a growing church. That particular day, "Doug", our church's youth leader, needed a baby-sitter for a few hours, so I was going to baby-sit his two kids for him.

We were all feeling hot and sweaty, so before Doug left, the kids asked if while he was gone we could all walk down the street to get some ice cream.

Doug said, "OK, sure. There's some money in a tin on the top shelf of the closet in my room. Just go in there and take what you need."

After he left, I went into the bedroom and opened the closet. I guess I picked up the wrong tin, because when I opened it I was totally surprised and shocked to find *marijuana* instead of money. I could smell it, and I knew right away what it was. I just stood there with my mouth open. I didn't know what to think, or what I should do.

I remembered how Doug was always telling our youth group not to do drugs. We had even had a big "Say 'No' to Drugs" program just a few weeks earlier. Suddenly I felt like Doug was a big liar and a hypocrite. But then I immediately thought about how I'd always looked up to him and how sincere he had always seemed to be.

A million emotions were pumping through me. I was upset and confused by my thoughts about what I believed was wrong and my feelings of loyalty to someone I considered to be a leader and a friend. I didn't want to get Doug in trouble because he seemed to be a good youth leader, but I knew what he was doing wasn't right. I felt totally mixed up about what to do.

A whole miserable week went by and then a few more days. Every day I felt worse and worse. I felt guilty about not telling anyone what I knew, but I just couldn't bring myself to tell the truth and maybe get Doug in a lot of trouble. I prayed over and over and asked God for the answer, but for a while I still didn't know what I should do.

Finally I told my friend, Sandy, what had happened. Sandy said, "I think you've just got to tell your dad." I believed she was right, but the thought of actually doing it was really hard for me. I liked Doug and I liked his family. I prayed about the situation some more.

When I talk to God, which is pretty much all the time, He seems to give me little signs about what I should do. Sometimes, He gives me that little "knowing feeling" inside my heart about what's right or wrong. I said, "Oh God, please tell me what to do."

It seemed like God heard me and answered my prayer. I decided to tell my dad what had happened by writing the whole thing in a letter. Even though my dad and I are really close, this way seemed easier for me. I could explain it better in writing than I could by just saying the words. I went to the living room and gave him the letter. Then I sat there watching him while he read it. I felt so bad about it that I started crying while he was reading.

The next day, my dad called Doug into his office and talked to him. Later, I was shocked to find out Doug had resigned and he and his family were moving to Wisconsin. I was really sad about that and I knew it was all my fault. I had felt guilty before because I hadn't spoken up, but now I felt twice as guilty because I had!

My dad could see that I was having a hard time with all this, so he talked to me and told me I had done the right thing. When I thought it over, I said, "Yeah, I did the right thing, but I still feel bad about it and I probably always will."

To make matters worse, Sandy was upset that Doug was leaving and so she was mad at me.

Sandy was the first friend I had made when we moved to this community. Even though she was the one who said I should tell my dad, she hadn't expected that Doug would leave. The main reason Sandy was mad at me was that she was "best buddies" with Doug's son, Zack—she really liked him a lot. They always hung out. Now Zack and his family had to move away and, of course, Sandy was blaming me.

It's been a few years since it happened, but I still feel guilty every time I think about Zack, even though I know I did the right thing. Making the right choice and doing what God tells you to do is sometimes pretty hard. But when I think of what could have happened to some of the other kids, or to Doug's own kids—if he kept on being a youth leader and using illegal drugs—I just know I did the right thing.

I believe Doug probably learned a valuable lesson from this experience. I'm hoping so, and feel pretty sure that this made him realize his mistake and want to change his actions.

I'm so grateful that I have a close relationship with both my parents. I thank God I can tell them what's bothering me. Most of my friends can't do that with their parents. I'm lucky. Most of my friends have parents who are divorced. Because things are rough at home, they just aren't comfortable talking to their parents.

If I were giving advice, I'd tell kids to do what you know is right even if it seems hard to do. I'd tell kids to find someone they can trust—a pastor or good friend, a grandparent—just anyone who really cares about you, who cares about what's right and who will listen. Talk things over with that person, but don't forget to pray too.

I think about what could have happened if someone other than me had found the pot. Someone else might have taken it and started experimenting with it. All kinds of bad things could have happened. When I look at all the things that could have happened, I'm so glad I did the right thing. God was leading me and I'm glad I was listening.

God is always there for us. We just need to tell Him the problem and ask for His help.

*Editor's Note: Except for the author's name, all names in this story have been changed.*

MacKenzie Bennett is a member of her high school swim team and water polo team. In addition to her school activities, she is an avid surfer. She is active in many ministries at the church pastored by her father.

# It's Too Soon to Quit!

## Jennifer Cramp
## with Neva B. True

I was born in Oregon in 1980 with a lung disease called cystic fibrosis. My parents had never heard of such a disease. The doctor told them it is fatal and there is no cure. It affects not only the lungs, but also the digestive system. Life expectancy, he said, would be three to four years.

Since then, medical research has found new treatments for this disease. From three or four years, life expectancy went to a fifty/fifty chance of becoming a teenager. By the time I was eight it had increased to eighteen years. It continues to go up.

Starting school was extra special for me. From kindergarten through third grade I went to a Christian school, and from fourth through eighth grade I was in public school. I wanted to do my best work—but it wasn't easy when I was sick a lot.

New hope filled my high school years. *A teenager and still alive!* Even the name of the school was New Hope.

But during my junior year that hope was really tested. I missed months of school at a time. It was stressful trying to make up school work, keep up my grade point average and have a social life. Keeping up with my friends, going to basketball games and practicing with the softball team were often impossible. Sometimes I was disappointed when I couldn't go on activities or stay out late.

Instead, I required extra sleep or had to have an intravenous injection. These started at birth. For my first ten years I spent much of my time in the hospital having IVs. Then, in 1990, a port-a-cath (a catheter that allows me to do my own IV at home) was implanted in my chest.

Besides the port-a-cath, I had a tube put in my stomach in 1992. Once a week it has to be flushed out—this is not pleasant, but it is necessary. When I get an ordinary cold it usually turns into a strain of pneumonia that spreads from my lungs to other parts of my body. Without antibiotics it could be fatal.

So you see, having cystic fibrosis upsets much of what would be normal for most kids. Being with others who have the same disease and understand helps a lot. Every summer for about seven years I went to a camp for kids with cystic fibrosis. It was so much fun! We got to know each other and help one another.

There was much diversity at the camp, but everyone had cystic fibrosis and we all accepted one another. The only sad thing was that each new summer some of our friends would have died since the last camp. I missed them.

I'm glad I trusted Jesus as my Savior when I was a small child. He never leaves me and is always with me as my Friend and Helper. I've reaffirmed my faith in Him as I've grown older.

I do not get angry at God, but sometimes I get angry at my situation. It is frustrating and upsetting. I have been dealing with that ever since I was born. I still don't know how to deal with it, but it's a growing experience. I remember coming to my all-time lowest point. Lying in the hospital bed I started questioning, "Why is it like this? Why does it keep going? I can't do this anymore."

At this hardest moment in my life, I prayed. Immediately I felt the Holy Spirit in the room and Jesus at my side saying, "It will be OK." That was the coolest experience for me. Ever since then when people ask me if I've ever felt the presence of the Holy Spirit, I always tell them about that special time.

One of my favorite Bible verses is First Peter 5:10 which says, "And after you have suffered a little while, the God of all grace, who has called you to his eternal glory in Christ, will himself restore, establish, and strengthen you" (RSV).

This promise helped me look at my disease as a blessing, not a problem. I honestly don't think I'd be as close to Christ if I didn't have cystic fibrosis. So, from that aspect I'm thankful for this trial. I think that's probably one of the reasons God gave it to me—to draw me closer to Him and help others do the same.

When I go to the doctor I watch for someone in the waiting room that I can encourage. That may be the whole reason I am supposed to go. Sometimes I don't know why things are happening and I may not know until I get to heaven. Then I'll find out the lives I've touched for God as He worked through me.

I think being part of a research project for new treatments for cystic fibrosis is another way God let me help others. For two years I went to Portland, Oregon for these trial testings. I like being part of God's big picture.

When my parents learned of my condition and the doctor's prognosis at the time of my birth, they didn't know what was going to happen; but they chose to always be there for me if I made it. For that I am forever thankful. I'm also grateful for the medical research that has found new treatments for this disease and has extended my life.

My parents, family and friends have helped me in so many ways. They are great examples to follow. I remember times when I wasn't up to talking and they would come in, sit down and just cheer me up by being there. Something from God's Word always helped. When I don't know where to look in the Bible for what I need, I use a concordance for words like *comfort* or *hope*. He has lots of surprises for me.

One of God's greatest surprise blessings has been for me to be able to go to college. For years I dreamed of living long enough to attend. And now I'm going back to the very area where I went to camp: I am enrolled in a Christian college in Salem, Oregon.

I am really excited and thankful. The college staff knows about my particular situation and is working with me to meet my special needs. I know I'll make it there too because the God of impossibilities is with me and for me.

It's always too soon to quit, until I graduate to heaven.

> *Author's note:* In five years of knowing her, I've seen this young lady repeatedly bounce back from impossible odds. She has inspired me as I've observed her remarkable ways of living an unbelievable life.
>
> I asked Jennifer's permission to record her awesome life story so I could share it with others. Being modest, she did not mention the honors she has received: the newspaper articles about her, being Student Body President, being on the all-star softball team or finishing as runner-up in the Sweet Sixteen Beauty Contest. I have told you her story as she told it to me. The words are from her heart to yours, especially for those of you who may be going through hurts and trials right now.
>
> —Neva B. True

Jennifer Cramp

Neva B. True and her pastor husband live in Grants Pass, Oregon. They are blessed with three children and six grandchildren. As a Titus 2 lady, she loves serving the Lord and others by leading Bible studies, speaking and writing. Her ministries have also included youth work and music. Neva is a graduate of Wheaton College in Christian Education. She is also a published author of articles for a Christian magazine and has written a devotional book.

## *Christmas in July*

## *Rudy Galdonik*

Christmas 1994 promised to bring the usual excitement and joy for fourteen-year-old David Neff—family traditions, drinking eggnog by the fire, a Christmas Eve candlelight church service, gifts lovingly wrapped and placed under the tree. Living in East Greenwich, Rhode Island with his parents and fifteen-year-old sister, Katie, David always considered Christmas his favorite time of the year.

But this year things were different. Torrential rains and winds pounded their fury at the Neff's ranch house tucked among the tall pines at the edge of town. As the storm continued to rage, a power outage cut off all electricity to the house.

Since they relied on electricity for everything including heat and well water, the Neff family had to decide how to get ready for their annual church Christmas Eve supper and service—now only hours away.

133

Close friends, who were out of town for the holidays, had left their house key with the Neffs, who decided they could shower at their friends' house and still make it to the service.

Just as they were ready to head over to church, Katie realized she had forgotten the shoes she had planned to wear that night. Her dad drove her back to their house to pick up her shoes and then over to the church to join David and their mom.

The service was wonderful. Full of smiles and Christmas joy, friends and fellow parishioners celebrated the special night. After the service, since the Neffs had arrived in two separate cars, David and his dad decided to head home while his mom and sister continued to visit and wish people well.

As their car rounded the corner in front of their house, a shocking sight greeted them. Fire trucks, with flashing lights reflecting off the wet leaves of nearby trees, filled their driveway. Heavy gray smoke filled the air. As the car pulled to a stop at the end of the driveway, David jumped from the car and ran toward the house. Trembling, he ran to a fireman standing nearby.

"Where's my dog?" he screamed.

The look of sorrow on the fireman's face told David that his six-year-old golden retriever, Digger, had not survived the fire. Digger was gone. Both Pepper, the old family cat and a tiny kitten that had been a family Christmas gift only the week before, had also died. Much of the interior of their home was either gone or heavily damaged  by smoke and water.

The car carrying David's mom and sister pulled up. They ran up to the house where David stood trying to absorb the sight before him. A quick glance showed a gaping hole that once was the wall of Katie's bedroom. When Katie saw it she gasped. On her trip back home to retrieve her shoes she had lit a candle in her room—a candle that, in her rush, she had forgotten to blow out.

Since by this time the fire had been put out, the family was escorted into the house by one of the firemen. With tears streaming down their cheeks, the Neffs clutched at each other, trying to comprehend what they saw. As they stepped into a place that only hours before had been cozy and familiar, they smelled the stench of smoke. A thick black layer of soot and ashes coated everything in sight.

They slowly worked their way from room to room, noticing that nothing had escaped the horrible blackness of the soot. Katie's room was the most severely damaged; water still dripped from the furniture that had not been burnt.

When they came to the kitchen, David stopped abruptly when he got to the door. There, etched into what was once bright kitchen linoleum, was a perfect stencil in the black soot outlining the exact spot where Digger had died. David knew this sight would never leave him. For him, Christmas would never again be the same.

As weeks turned to months the Neff family slowly began to put the pieces of their lives back together. The insurance company would eventually replace the possessions that were lost. A trailer was moved into the yard next to the house for the family to live in. Friends and neighbors donated items for their use. Even David's anger toward his sister—for leaving the candle burning—slowly diminished. He had to admit it had been an accident—just an unfortunate accident.

A trip to the breeder introduced David to his new dog, Buddy, whose gangly energy soon filled David with new love and loyalty. But when Christmas 1995 came, it was filled with memories of the previous year and David again grieved for all he had lost.

One month later David received a challenging invitation: "How would you like to travel to Mexico this summer and build a house for a homeless family?"

At first David chuckled and dismissed the prospect. But then he rethought this far-fetched idea: Spending a week of his summer vacation to travel with other youth to a foreign country to do something good for a family of strangers sounded cool.

He agreed to join nine other teens from his town on this mission project. The youth mission group spent the spring months preparing for the trip. Finally the day arrived. Riding in a tattered school bus from a camp in Texas where the teens would live for a week, they watched out the windows as the bus turned into a *colonia,* or neighborhood, just outside the border town of Reynosa, Mexico.

The poverty that greeted them was beyond David's comprehension. Running from shacks made of scraps of cardboard, metal and wood, children with smiling faces and outstretched arms began to greet the teens.

The group from Rhode Island was assigned a dusty plot of dirt surrounded by barbed wire where they would build a twelve-by-sixteen-foot wooden shack. There was no electricity in the whole neighborhood, and the only water was provided by a faucet located down the street.

As David began to carry precut lumber to his group's site, he began to reflect back on that Christmas just a year and a half earlier, when he too had no electricity and no possessions. He quickly realized how truly fortunate he was. These people lived without the possessions he often took for granted, yet they seemed to be filled with joy. David became aware that God was teaching him some deep lessons as he hammered alongside his friends and played with the neighborhood children.

He began to understand that it is *truly* better to give than to receive. He learned that by trusting God when times are tough and then doing something good for someone else, we can grow and work through our own hard times. And that gift, when it's something the recipient can't possibly pay back, has even more meaning. It leaves the giver with a lasting sense of inner peace and joy.

It felt like Christmas in July.

A member of National Speakers Association, Rudy Galdonik uses humor as she tells of harrowing and sometimes tragic experiences in her own life, and encourages audiences to put a new perspective on the joys and struggles of life. Every year, she leads a group of teens to Mexico to build houses for homeless families.

E-mail: CanaryCom@aol.com
Fax: 401-885-4508

# Climbing a Ladder to Freedom

## "Josie"
### with Charlotte Huskey

I tried to escape into the bedroom. My friend Rhonda followed me.

"Talame says you'll squeal on us," she said. "He'll hurt me if you don't try what he brought. Take a little for me, OK?"

I had promised myself to stay clear of drugs. My dad headed a drug gang and I had seen the enslaving power of drugs, but to protect my friend, I tried some.

That did it—I was hooked.

One month later I stayed high four days and four nights. Sometime after that, I left home and bunked with a man who promised me drugs. I ended up in a juvenile hall and was placed in a group home for troubled teens.

Ethel and Clem Dixon, directors of the group home in which I had been placed, have been helping me climb a ladder to freedom, one rung at a time.

"You must attend school while staying in this home," Mrs. Dixon told me.

"I'm too far behind and too old," I said.

"You're never to old to learn," she said.

"I dropped out halfway through my freshman and sophomore years," I protested. "I probably have no credits."

"We'll see," she replied firmly. "Let's go."

I found that I had less than one-fifth of the credits needed for graduation. I didn't see how it was possible to catch up. But Mrs. Dixon continued to encourage me.

"The Bible says, 'I can do all things through Christ which strengtheneth me.' You can do it," she insisted.

The school counselor helped me design a schedule that would enable me to graduate in two years. It was a heavy load, but at the end of the first nine weeks, I brought home a report card with only A's and B's—quite different from those years when I would arrive at school half drunk, skip classes and try to lie my way out of trouble.

Boy, was I proud! And so were Ethel and Clem.

But I tended to slip back. Anger boiled deep inside me like a volcano ready to explode. It belched out every time Mrs. Dixon spoke to me. At the slightest provocation, I shouted, cursed, kicked or hit. I thought she was like my selfish, alcoholic mother—inconsiderate and bossy.

"You keep us here like prisoners only to earn money," I told her.

"I could find an easier way to make money," she answered, with a big smile. Her calmness in the face of my rudeness only baffled and irritated me more.

I had a lot of trouble with the other girls living at the home. My roommate, Santasha, and I would argue over trivial matters. While playing basketball with the boys from another group home, I fumbled the ball and Santasha called me "the 'b' word." Lowering my head, I started for her. We clawed, pulled hair and kicked. Two guys from the other group home forced us apart and held us. Of course we got written up, lost our privileges and had to see our counselors.

At school, I was a Red, and Stacy, another girl from the group home, was a Blue (gang names). "Keep away from my boyfriend," Stacy demanded.

"I wouldn't have such a runt," I shouted. She cursed me. I cursed her. Then I hit her and off to the school counselor we went.

Another girl, Claudia, had this drive to destroy things in the group home. She was also a Blue, and she hated my friends. We had trouble constantly. By then I had learned to respect Mrs. Dixon and her staff; when I heard big-mouthed Claudia talking bad about them, I slapped her—hard. Startled, she shrank back and shut her mouth.

Alcohol has been the hardest thing for me to get free from. Drugs, alcohol and being torn between divorced parents who fought over me just to hurt each other created a painful childhood. Although my mother didn't know it, I became dependent on alcohol at a young age.

I recently went home for a weekend and I started slipping back into my old habits. Instead of raining harsh words on me, Mrs. Dixon extended the protection I needed. "You will stay here with us until you get stronger," she said.

Ethel and Clem Dixon proved by their actions that it pays to trust in Christ. I became a Christian in September of 1997. Attending church regularly helps me, but most of my help comes from God whom I have learned to trust.

The Dixons have been the parents I needed. They lift me up when I'm down. They praise me when I do well, and they are always there when I need them. They arranged a meeting with both my parents and helped me to know how to express my true feelings toward them. That has started a healing process, and I am now able to forgive them.

When I had drug withdrawal symptoms or nightmares, Clem, who had once been on drugs, understood and helped me. Often he would say, "You're doing great," or "You can do it."

And I did.

My whole life has changed. I have been clean of drugs for more than a year now. I rarely get angry, and when I do I am usually able to keep my actions under control. If I continue according to schedule, I will be graduating from high school next spring. God truly has forgiven me for my failures and is strengthening me for the future.

The higher I climb on the ladder, the more freedom I have.

Charlotte Huskey, missionary and Christian educator, has had hundreds of Bible lessons and stories for children and young adults published in English and Spanish. For thirteen years she was editor of *The Beautiful Way,* a Sunday school handout. A mother of six, (five of whom are in full-time Christian service), she is in demand as a bilingual speaker on child development and home life. Charlotte and her husband live in Chapultepec, Baja California, Mexico. Besides regular missionary duties, they write, teach and translate.

E-mail: jahuskey@telnor.net

## Section 3

## My Own Special Teenage Kid

*For the* LORD *will again rejoice over thee for good.*
> (Deuteronomy 30:9, KJV)

The stories in this section tell how these adults lived through and coped with the ups and downs of a teenager under their care. Some went through the valleys along with their teenager. As a result, both the parent (or other caregiver) and the teenager grew wiser, stronger and closer to each other—not in spite of but *because* of the challenges they experienced and overcame together.

You will find inspiration in these true stories of challenges overcome and relationships rebuilt with God's help.

# Does This Count as Hospitality?

## Andria Anderson

Internally, I was raging. I knew there was no way I would complete the Bible application assignment. The assignment had to do with extending hospitality. Should I invite a neighbor over for conversation? Consulting my stuffed schedule, there was no way I could find the time. I felt like a failure.

Then, instead of a neighbor, God sent a teenage African-American male to my doorstep at 2 a.m. He was flanked by two police officers.

His name was Dan, and he was afraid to go home. My son, Jason, hadn't pried into Dan's home situation, but he suspected Dan's mother had kicked him out of the house. Dan had been living out of his backpack for a few months, often finding a party where he could linger until daybreak. Failing that, a friend might offer him a place to sleep for a night. He had slept in Jason's room several times.

Comparing Dan with our son, Jason, who lives in a stable two-parent family, yields irony. Dan may be homeless, but he is clean-cut. He always wears nice slacks and a button-down shirt. Jason, on the other hand, wears thrift shop clothes creatively altered with strategic slashes. Dan's hair is close cut; my son's is a green Mohawk. Somehow, the differences in personal expression put no damper on their friendship.

That night, when my sleep was disturbed by the cops pounding on my door, Dan had been waiting for Jason on our front porch. Jason had arranged to meet Dan about 2 a.m., but had forgotten and was staying overnight at another friend's house. Our neighbors had called the police to report a strange man lurking around our home.

After assuring the officers that Dan belonged here, I wondered: *Does* this *count as hospitality?* If so, God was playing loose with the assignment book.

Dan spent several nights, without police escort, in Jason's room. A few weeks later, the pounding on my front door in the middle of the night turned out to be Dan *again*. I'll admit to the brief thought, *The hospitality assignment was for* one *week, Lord.*

Trying to speak, small sobs escaped Dan's lips. I quickly bundled him into the house. "They beat me up," he gasped in a pained whisper. "They kept hitting me."

A group of drunks in their early twenties had used Dan for sport. Thankfully, he wasn't bleeding, but I told him to wake me up if blood showed up anywhere.

Dan's health declined over the next two days. I felt heartsick that I couldn't take him to our family doctor, but I wasn't his parent. I couldn't authorize medical treatment. A friend suggested County Hospital. We sent him off with money for the subway and prayers for his health.

A few hours later, a doctor at the hospital called. Dan had given our name and address as his home. As much as we cared, we weren't his parents. Dan would have to give his mother's information. Hearing no further word from Dan all that evening, I called the hospital and learned that someone with a car had picked him up.

We spent three days wondering what had happened. During those three days, we all came to the same conclusion. It was harder work worrying what this kid was doing next than it would be to have him live here! We agreed to offer Dan our home as a permanent residence. I felt so proud that Jason, who had only recently gotten a bedroom of his own, was willing to share it with Dan. I felt equally proud of my husband and two younger children, who agreed to disrupt their lives to add another person to the household.

Personally, I packaged up my concerns and asked God to store them away somewhere in case I chickened out.

The third day after the hospital had identified
and treated a massive strep infection in Dan's
throat, he was back, practicing my son's bass
guitar in our basement. Dan loved music and
practiced piano, bass or drums whenever the
chance arose.

"Could I talk with you a minute, Dan?" I asked.

"Sure!"

"Would you like to live in our house permanently? I mean, use this as your address and
leave your belongings here? And plan on sleeping here every night?"

Dan grinned with such relief and thankfulness
that I risked hugging him. He hugged me back—
hard.

As part of our agreement with Dan, he paid
rent by doing chores, applying for jobs now that
he had an address to put on applications, and attending church with us each Sunday—no matter
how late he had been out on Saturday night. We
were afraid he'd find church boring, but he
loved the band, the singing and the preaching.
He dug out a tiny Bible a friend had given him
and began to read it. He soaked up God's Living
Water like a dying plant.

One evening, standing in our kitchen, I explained a prayer for salvation. Dan enthusiasti-
cally prayed it for his soul. "Father, I've sinned
against You and against other people. I can do
nothing to help make up for those sins. Jesus,
You are the Redeemer of souls, the only Savior
from sin. I need You to be my Savior. Holy

Spirit, please enter into my heart and life and direct my path from now on."

Dan now bags groceries at a local grocery store, and he's quick to agree to as many overtime hours as he can get. He will restart his junior year of high school in the fall. He cheerfully completes his chores. He regularly causes my husband and me to smirk when he jibes our children for griping about the hardships in their home life. The turnaround in his life is inspiring.

However, it has not all been smooth going. The police called one night at 1:30 a.m. They had delivered Dan to the hospital, tripped out on acid. Tied to the gurney with restraints, Dan suffered equally from embarrassment that Jason and I were seeing him like that and amazement that we would come sit with him all those hours. He lucked out this time: Children's Services didn't take him away.

Once home, Dan's head hung so low that I feared for his neck. For days, he wouldn't look at me or join in a conversation. When I finally had a talk with him, he said, "When I used to do this stuff, I knew it was wrong, but I never felt bad about it. This time I *feel* bad—really bad."

Maybe watching the birth pangs of a conscience shouldn't be funny, but I had to bite my cheeks to keep from grinning. Entirely too well acquainted myself with the Holy Spirit's prickling, I warned Dan, "It doesn't get any easier, either. God's not satisfied until you're *holy*."

So far, offering hospitality to God's odd choice for a guest has paid back more than it has cost. We pray for His strength if the way becomes more rocky. God has given Dan a new base for his life, and we suspect there are amazing events ahead of him.

As for me, I'm not so worried about Bible application assignments any more.

Andria Anderson lives in Chicago with her husband, three children and foster teens. Years of inner-city teaching developed her concern and caring for deprived children. She divides her time between writing, restoring their large Victorian home and attempting to count how many teens currently live there.

E-mail: AAnder87@aol.com.

## One Bounce at a Time

### *Nancy I. Pamerleau*

One bitterly cold February night in northern Michigan, the snow was flying and the thermostat had dropped well below zero. Casey told his mother that he was spending the night with a friend to do homework. He lied. Instead, he spent that Thursday evening driving the country roads in his car, drinking with two friends.

Casey was angry. His dad had moved out of their nice family home right after Christmas. There had always been a lot of fighting in the house. Casey fought with his dad, and his parents fought with each other—mostly about him.

In a way, Casey felt responsible for his dad's leaving. He stayed with his mother because he felt she needed his support. She was trying to hold down a job and manage the division of property and the sale of the house—and she cried a lot.

153

She also prayed a lot for her son. So did her friends. She had taken him to church for all of his sixteen years, and she knew that under all that rebellion there was a good kid.

Long before the divorce began, Casey was picked up by the police. He drank, smoked and hung out with the wrong crowd; then he *became* the wrong crowd. The bitter divorce only made his need for alcohol and drugs seem greater. His addictions and his anger pulled him deeper and deeper into an underworld that seemed inescapable.

On this particular Thursday night he was halfway between two little villages. Nothing but woods lay along that fifteen mile stretch. The car sputtered, then died. Casey and his friends coasted to a stop. They were out of gas.

At twenty degrees below zero, no heat, a seven-mile walk for gas in either direction, and too much alcohol to reason well, the threat of freezing to death was quite real.

At home his mother had prayed and gone to sleep at 10:00, thinking he was safe at his friend's house. At 11:30 she awoke suddenly, as if someone had shaken her. She immediately got out of bed, fell to her knees and began praying for Casey.

At 1:30 the phone rang. It was the police. They had arrested Casey after finding him and his friends at 11:30—the very moment she had awakened and prayed.

Casey spent the night in jail for driving under the influence, driving with an open intoxicant and a couple of other charges. Since he was also on antidepressants, they were concerned that he was suicidal, so a volunteer sat with him all night to keep watch. It wasn't just the volunteer that kept watch that night. Being arrested probably saved Casey's life. God was looking out for him, even in his rebellion.

Casey continued down that same road. He seemed bent on self-destruction. He got drunk and high, disappeared for days and missed more days of school than he attended. He had so much trouble at school that the principal had his mother's phone number on speed dial. In fact, Casey accumulated so many detentions that he wasn't allowed to walk in the graduation ceremony. And if he didn't complete his detention time by June 13 at 3:00 p.m., the week after graduation, he wouldn't get a diploma. He finished his detention time at 2:30 p.m. on that day.

He had bounced back temporarily.

Casey had a couple more brushes with the law and several with death. Four of his friends died in less than three years. More than that went to jail. But his mother kept praying that God would keep him alive and draw him back to Him.

By the time he was arrested a second time, both of Casey's parents had remarried. When the day came for him to go before the judge, his stepfather went with him while his mother stayed home and prayed again.

Casey, for a change, was clean-shaven and neat when he went before the judge, his long hair pulled back into a braided ponytail and tucked down the collar of his sport jacket. He decided to level with the judge about his problem rather than to be sulky and evasive. The judge gave him a year's probation.

Walking out of the courtroom with them, the probation officer said he was totally amazed at the judge's decision. Before the hearing the judge had said he was going to send Casey to prison for a year because he was out of high school and a repeat offender.

The probation officer couldn't figure out what had changed the judge's mind. Casey's mother knew: It was prayer. God was watching over Casey.

God deals with us in different ways. Just as God created every snowflake with a different pattern, He likewise created us as individuals and deals with us that way. Bouncing back doesn't usually happen overnight and it usually isn't easy. But though Casey felt hopelessly snared and expected to die young, he continued to seek God's help, while his mother never stopped praying for him.

Today, Casey has been through two years of college and has learned skills that helped him find a well-paying job. He has been able to drag himself out of the bondage of drugs with the help of a friend, which is an answer to his mother's prayers. And he has been able to forgive his father because, as he said, "I can't hate him forever."

Of course, pumping drugs, cigarettes and alcohol into his body over a period of seven years has taken its toll, but Casey is rebuilding his life—one bounce at a time.

Nancy I. Pamerleau is a full-time Interpersonal and Public Communication instructor at Kirtland Community College in Roscommon, Michigan. She is a frequent speaker for Christian and professional organizations, and has authored numerous articles and stories for professional journals and magazines such as *Virtue* and *Discipleship Journal*. She is Casey's mom.

E-mail: pamerlen@k2.kirtland.cc.mi.us

## Eighteen and Rebellious

### Florence Littauer

When my daughter Marita was eighteen and in a rebellious stage, I determined to pour my life into her in such a way that she would want to stay in the fold. I told her daily how much I loved her and what a joy she was to my life. I did not criticize her clothes or companions, and I made all her friends welcome in our home. I took her with me on speaking trips and, while she appeared uninterested in what I was teaching, the words were going into her mental computer. She liked the excitement of traveling, and she accepted "listening to Mother" as paying her way.

Once I said to her, "I can envision the two of us speaking together: you doing outer beauty and me doing inner beauty." Years later she reminded me of my statement and let me know what her reaction had been at the time. She had made no comment then but had said to herself,

"That will be the day when I spend my time in churches with women!"

We continued to spend our time in churches with women. Marita listened to my speaking, Bible teaching and counseling. At the end of each day I would go over the life stories of the different women and ask her what she thought each should do to overcome her problems. Whatever she came up with as an answer, I would compliment her on her sound thinking.

One day she announced, "I want to travel with you all the time. What should I do to get ready?"

Marita had always had an eye for color. Her college courses were in design, and she had become a sharp and stylish dresser. We found customized training for her, and she became a color consultant. When I was asked to speak at women's retreats, I would volunteer Marita as a special feature on fashion, and they would be glad to get a free bonus. As she spoke to women, I would evaluate her performance. She had a teachable spirit, and soon her ability moved from adequate to above average.

When she was twenty and in business for herself, Marita told me, "When I'm doing color consultations with ladies, they start telling me their marriage problems, and I'm just amazed at the answers I give them. I've never been married, and yet I open my mouth and out comes the right advice. Then I realize it's your words, Mother, that I'm saying. It's my mouth, but it's your advice. Those years of filling me up have paid off."

How grateful I am that Marita has stored up more information from her Christian mother than from atheistic professors. The Bible tells us that when we as "virtuous women" have done what we should do, our children will rise up and call us blessed (Proverbs 31:28). Marita has chosen to follow in my footsteps, and that is blessing enough for me.

Marita is in her thirties now and married. She speaks at churches, businesses and writers' conferences, and is the director of marketing for CLASS (Christian Leaders and Speakers Seminars).* She has even followed in my footsteps by writing four books (even though she had no interest in writing high school compositions).

Never underestimate the power you have to program the computer mind in your child. What you put in will later come out. One day when Fred and I took our nine-year-old grandson Bryan out shopping, we drove into a superstore parking lot. Bryan spoke up.

"We should not trade in that store. They come into towns, sell at low prices and put others out of business. It's not fair to the small businessman who's working hard to make a living." Where did this little speech come from? Was he reading the *Wall Street Journal*, or did he hear his father and mother talking about the effects of that superstore chain on their small business? We may not ever know they're listening because they don't seem to hang on our every word. They don't even want us to know they've heard what we've said, but they have. Keep feeding the machine.

"Train up a child in the way he should go: and when he is old, he will not depart from it" (Proverbs 22:6, KJV).

*\*Editor's Note: Marita Littauer became President of CLASS in 1997.*

From *It Takes So Little to Be Above Average* by Florence Littauer. © 1996 Harvest House Publishers, Eugene, OR. Used by permission.

Florence Littauer, founder of CLASS (Christian Leaders, Authors and Speakers Seminars, Inc.), is a best-selling author of over twenty-five books. With her husband Fred she travels nationally and internationally as a Christian speaker, sharing her humor and valuable insights. Florence is also in demand as a radio and TV talk show guest and keynote speaker for retreats, business conventions and seminars. Between their travels, Florence and Fred reside in Palm Springs, California.

# From the Pit
## to the Pathway

## Carol S. Miller

I was dropping my daughter off at the university. Before she got out of the car I felt I had to talk to her once again about how she was destroying her life.

"Cici, listen to me," I said. "God is the answer to what's going on in your life! No matter how much you want to deny it, He's the only answer. You've tried everything else and look what's happened to you!"

Her face flushed with anger. "Mom, why is it that every time we talk about my problems, you have to bring God into it? Can't you ever leave Him out?"

"No, Cici, I can't—because God is the only way out of the pit you're in!"

Cici flung open the door, slammed it behind her and stormed back to her dorm. So ended another of our seemingly fruitless mother-daughter conversations.

I prayed all the way home from the university that day. *Dear Jesus, please help her. You're the only One who can save her from all this. Please save her, Lord!*

I couldn't help but wonder how this could have ever happened to my precious child. It wasn't always like that. God had blessed us with this energetic and animated child who was now a young woman. All through her early childhood, she and I had wonderful times, first playing, later talking about dreams, school, boys and friends, sharing all the trials and triumphs of her life.

How could I have missed seeing the changes that now were so evident? The changes were hardly anything out of the ordinary, I thought—certainly to be expected in adolescence. But when I saw her school picture, the radical appearance and forlorn look set off an alarm deep within me. I suddenly realized that the dramatic makeup, the drastic hairstyles, the bursts of excitement and happiness one moment, seclusion and hopelessness the next—changes that I thought were normal for adolescent girls—were anything but normal. Something was definitely wrong!

We sought professional help. The symptoms were analyzed and the diagnosis given—Bipolar Disorder, a major affective disorder that is characterized by episodes of mania and depression.

Depression was a familiar term to our family. I had experienced its clutches a year or so earlier. Bipolar, we didn't know. What we did know was that our daughter was in a great struggle, a struggle that began with manic-depression and led through the valley of drug abuse and even suicide attempts.

Bipolar Disorder is like a ball and chain that entangles a person in confusion and fear. Cici tried to escape the life she hated. Her suicide attempts failed, praise God! Running away from home didn't help—she couldn't run away from herself. Hiding behind weird makeup and wild hairstyles only heightened the isolation she felt. The more we tried to reach her, the farther away she seemed to be.

My prayers continued: *Dear Jesus, please help my child!*

Cici turned to drugs—marijuana, cocaine, anything she could get—because she thought that would help her forget the past and escape the pain. Not so. While Bipolar is the ball and chain, drugs are the spikes that maim and kill. Drugs made the mania and depression worse, which made her want to escape more. Was there no end to this nightmare?

It went on through junior high, high school and on into college. Even then, it wasn't over. The surroundings changed, but the situation remained. Cici tried so hard to help herself. She knew *about* Jesus, but she didn't yet *know* Him. I had shared with her about the Lord at every opportunity and I shared my testimony of healing with her, but her heart was so hardened the message never got through.

Then came that day at the university: shouting, a slammed door and storming off. I realized she wasn't running from me—she was running from the truth. I knew her problem was out of her control, and there was only One who could save her from destruction and death.

*Dear Jesus, please!*

I didn't realize He had already begun to answer.

"Mom! Mom! Guess what! *Guess what!*" Cici's excited words opened our conversation on the phone that night—that glorious night of divine intervention.

In a voice bubbling over with joy and exhilaration, Cici said the words that I will never forget: "I accepted Jesus as my Savior, Mom!"

We serve a mighty God who does fantastic works through those who are faithful and willing to serve Him. God had used my younger daughter, Sharon, to be His instrument. That afternoon, Cici, after much prodding, had attended Sharon's Bible study—not to learn about the Lord, but just to support her sister. It was there that Jesus reached down, opened Cici's heart and saved her soul. Cici responded to the Lord's grace with such joy, she just *had* to call and tell me!

We laughed, we cried, we talked on the phone for over an hour. Tears of gratitude, joy and relief flowed from both of us that night! Cici expressed the freedom and that "joy unspeakable" that only Jesus can give.

"I feel so light, Mom!" was the way she described the burden lifted from her.

Ever since that moment when Cici was brought out of the pit and placed on the pathway to heaven, she has been on fire for Jesus. She is consumed by finding the truth, soaking up the Word and seeking His will for her life. She has testified to His power, bowed to His holiness and she lives to see Him glorified.

The gifts He gave her at birth are being used in service to our Savior. The traits that the enemy tried to use for her destruction are being used for God's glory. She works for the Lord no matter where He puts her. She knows she can do all things God calls her to do, for she knows her strength is in Christ. She boldly speaks truth, and her excitement and animation reveal her joy.

Roman 8:28 says, "And we know that in all things God works for the good of those who love him, who have been called according to his purpose." Cici and I can testify to the truth of that. We *know*, without a single doubt, that in *all* things—the good, the bad and the ugly—God does work for our good when we love Him and are called according to His purpose. Learning through her experiences, Cici is able to relate with compassion to others who are suffering; she has the ability to listen and share her testimony to the hope that is within her. Through her testimony, God is revealed and glorified.

Again and again God proves His faithfulness. He sees us as what He will bring us to be, not for what we are now. Turning our trials to triumphs, in all things He works for our good and for His glory. He has, He does and He will!

As a speaker, Carol Sargent Miller encourages her audiences to step up with conviction, step forward with confidence and step in stride with Jesus. She lives life with enthusiasm and delivers humorous, humbling life-lessons in presentations to youth groups, Christian women's groups, ministers' conferences and women's retreats.

Address: 12315 Streamvale Circle, Herndon, VA 20170
E-mail: Hapinhar@aol.com

# Learning to Listen from the Heart

## Diana L. James

We met for the first time in the parking lot at the mall. I wore a flower in my hair and Jean wore a purple blouse so we could find each other, just as we had planned when we spoke on the phone. We sat down in a quiet corner of an almost empty café.

Jean appeared to be in her early forties. Her hair and clothes were stylish and attractive, but I noticed Jean's eyes were swollen and her nose was red, as if she had been crying—hard. She seemed so jumpy and nervous that I thought she might get up and run out the door at any moment.

I thought to myself, *No wonder she's nervous— she doesn't even know me. She's in deep distress about her daughter, and probably has no idea how I could help her or even why I'm here to try.*

My reassuring smile was somewhat nervous too. Jean was the first "helpee" I had been as-

169

signed to since completing my year of Stephen
Ministries training. Our church had sponsored
this highly respected, interdenominational training course to help with pastoral care. Several of us
met each week to learn how to share the love of
the Lord with those who are going through a crisis
in their lives. We studied about grief recovery, the
dynamics of family relationships and the reasons
families sometimes fall apart, the causes and cures
for stress, crisis intervention and other related
subjects. Much of the training was similar to
classes I had taken in college.

But there was a striking difference: The purpose
of Stephen Ministries is to share God's love with
the person in crisis. Most of our training centered
on learning to listen with intelligent compassion
and respond with genuine Christian love. When a
person called the church or pastor for help, they
were told about the Stephen Ministries program
and were asked if they would be willing to meet
with a "helper" who had graduated from the
course. I was one of those graduates and Jean had
called the church for help.

Jean and I took a few minutes getting acquainted—talking about the weather and other
trivia—before we both relaxed to the point where
I could bring up the subject we were there to dis-
cuss: Jean's sixteen-year-old daughter, Emily.

"Tell me about Emily," I suggested as gently
as I could.

"She's breaking my heart," Jean whispered hoarsely as a tear slipped down her cheek. "She says she hates me. Emily used to be such a sweet, obedient girl, a good student, active in sports and in our church's youth group. She's changed so much I don't know her anymore. She doesn't want to go to school or church. She lies to me, yells at me and has run away from home three times."

"Do you remember when you first noticed a change in her behavior?" I asked.

Jean thought for a moment. "I guess it was a few months after her dad moved out. He left almost a year ago. Emily didn't seem a bit upset when he left."

Jean talked about her husband, about Emily and about her other two younger children while I listened quietly. Sometimes it was hard for me not to comment or verbally sympathize. But I reminded myself of my training and I didn't offer any suggestions or advice—I just listened intently to all she said. I did pray a somewhat stumbling prayer for her and her family when an hour had passed and it was time for us to go our separate ways.

Driving home, I prayed again for Jean and Emily. I wondered if she would want to meet with me again or if it had all been too painful for her. I prayed that our meeting had helped Jean in at least some small way. We had tentatively agreed to meet again in two weeks, but when I called to verify our next meeting, I half expected her to make an excuse not to come.

She didn't. After that, we met every two weeks at the same time and place.

During the time between our meetings I studied the Stephen Ministries manual, reminding myself that I was not a counselor, not a doctor, not a psychologist, but just a sister in Christ trying to respond to Jean's need for Christian love and understanding.

Each time we met it seemed to me Jean was slightly stronger and less frantic and hopeless about Emily, even though Emily's behavior had certainly not improved. She was still cutting school, avoiding church, yelling at her mom and staying out overnight with her nonchurch friends without permission or adult supervision.

My somewhat awkward prayers for Emily, both in Jean's presence and when I was alone, became more and more fervent and heartfelt as I came to care deeply about their family and their situation. When we were together I encouraged Jean to join me in prayer, but she was shy and only said "Amen" at the end of my prayers.

During this time plans came together for my husband, Max, and me to sell our business and move to southern California, some 400 miles away. I reluctantly told Jean about this rather sudden turn of events. I gave her a little refrigerator magnet with a Scripture verse: "Trust in the LORD with all your heart and lean not on your own understanding" (Proverbs 3:5). I promised to continue to pray for Emily and the family. Thus ended our helper/helpee relationship.

Many big changes occurred and many months passed before I heard from Jean again. Her letter had been forwarded twice before it got to me. Sharp twinges of guilt jabbed at me as I opened Jean's letter. I felt I had abandoned her. I wondered if I had been any help to her at all. Actually, I felt I had failed her. I had broken my promise. In the busy course of moving and getting settled in our new location, I had hardly ever taken time to drop her a note, and only occasionally remembered to pray for her and for Emily.

As I unfolded her letter, two dozen sparkles of shimmering confetti spilled out. (And it wasn't even my birthday or New Year's Eve!) Happy smiley faces drawn in colored pencil and stickers reading "Praise the Lord" adorned the edges of the writing paper.

Jean's joy, love and appreciation overflowed.

"I cannot thank you enough, Diana, for what you did for me and for my family," she wrote. "You'll never know what our meetings and your beautiful prayers meant to me." As I read her words my eyes blurred with tears.

*I guess I didn't fail her after all!*

Jean explained that our times of praying together had given her strength and hope. Because of that, she had called upon God daily to help her deal with Emily. God had answered her prayers—Emily had returned to the Lord and had changed from being hostile to being loving toward her mom. She was back in school, getting good grades again, and had been voted assistant leader of the church youth group. Jean was overjoyed—and so was I!

Diana L. James' articles and stories have appeared in national magazines and in seven anthology books. She is author/editor/compiler of *Bounce Back* (1997) and *Bounce Back Too* (1998). Diana hosted a TV interview program for five years, was a member of National Speakers Association for five years and is on the teaching staff of CLASS (Christian Leaders, Authors, and Speakers Seminars, Inc.). She speaks for retreats, church groups and women's conferences. Diana and her husband, Max, live in Meridian, Idaho, near Boise.

E-mail:  DianaJames@aol.com

# Stitches

## *Patsy Clairmont*

The age span between our boys didn't keep them from big-time wrestling bouts. I pointed out to Jason that challenging his seventeen-year-old brother was not exactly wise. Jason seemed to have a Hulk Hogan mind-set but the body frame of Pee Wee Herman.

During a body slam attempt, he fell over a footstool and cut his head open on the corner of the wall. Les and I hustled Jason off to the emergency room because it was obvious he would need more than a Band-Aid®.

Jason was shaken and asked, "How bad is it?"

I realized that the location of his injury was to our advantage. He couldn't see it.

"Not real bad," I assured him.

"What are they going to do to me?"

Measuring my words, I responded, "Fix it."

"How?"

"They're going to put it back together again," I tried.

"How?" he pushed.

I'd run out of Humpty Dumpty stalls and decided to go for the direct approach.

"They're going to stitch that thing shut, Jason," I declared.

He gasped and then groaned. "Is it going to hurt?"

"Probably," I confessed.

"But what if it hurts more than I'm able to bear?" he pleaded.

"Then you'll reach down inside of you and pull up your courage. Because you accepted Jesus as your Savior, He assures us we can do all things through Christ who strengthens us. So if it hurts more than you can bear, you pray, and He will help you."

Jason became very quiet. We pulled up to the emergency entrance, and I took him in while Les parked the car. The doctor came in, took a look at Jason's injury and began to prepare the wound for sutures. Lest things get active, he had two nurses come in, one to stand on each side of Jason.

Halfway through the process, the doctor realized both nurses were not necessary since Jason offered no resistance. Not once did Jason object to the process or even ask the doctor to stop.

One of the nurses turned to leave when she noticed someone else in the room who was in need of help. I'm not sure if it was my magenta and jade skin tone or my swaying in the breeze that alerted her, but she guided me to a chair and began to fan me. Later the doctor assisted me to the car.

On the way out he said, "I cannot tell you what a privilege it was to work on a boy like that."

My husband shot me a glance as if to say, "Wish I could say the same for his mother!"

As we drove home, I asked Jason, "Did it hurt so bad you had to pray?"

"Oh, Mom, I didn't wait. As soon as you told me, I prayed," he confessed.

"What a good idea. I . . . wish . . . I . . . would . . . have . . . thought of that," I whispered.

*Is your life sutured in prayer?*

Patsy Clairmont travels throughout the U.S. providing hope and humor for Christian retreats, luncheons, seminars and workshops. Currently, she is a featured speaker with the New Life Clinic's Women of Faith presentations. She is the author of several best-selling books and has two best-selling books that she wrote cooperatively with the other Women of Faith speakers. Patsy has just released her latest book, *Tea with Patsy Clairmont*. She and her husband, Les, live in Brighton, Michigan.

Web site: www.patsyclairmont.com

## Section 4

## What I Learned from Working with Teens

*We live by faith, not by sight.*
(2 Corinthians 5:7)

It is generally agreed that most teenagers feel more comfortable discussing their feelings with an "outsider" than they do with members of their own families.

Those who have contributed stories for this section are people who sincerely care about teenagers. They work with, or have worked with, teens on a regular basis. Some are, or have been, leaders of various types of youth groups, some are speakers who encourage teens through youth rallies and at youth camps, others have worked as youth pastors.

Because of their close contact with teens, and the opportunities they often have to talk and counsel one-on-one with them, these youth workers have insights that are frequently deeper than the understanding of most teachers and parents.

Many of those insights are revealed in the following true life stories and commentaries.

# Close Encounter

## Linda Shepherd

"Be careful what you pray for" should have been my instruction to the kids in my group when I was a summer youth director. It would have been, if I had known how dangerous getting what you pray for can be.

"Let's pray for a miracle," I had suggested to the young people at the small southwest Texas church where I worked during my summer break from Lamar University.

"Let's dream up a prayer that seems too big even for God—and let's see what He does with it."

Veronica, a tiny teenager with dark brown hair and eyes to match, raised her hand. "You've been teaching us how to tell people about Jesus," she said. "Let's pray God will give us the chance to witness to our town's gang leaders!"

I gulped, thinking of the tough brown-skinned teens who helped smuggle drugs over the Mexican border for the local crime syndicate.

"All right," I said, "why not? Let's pray we will get a chance to witness to Mundo and Manuel."

The young people bowed their heads and prayed earnestly. But despite our prayer for a miracle, I felt safe. These tough teens we were praying for were not likely to visit our church. And I was not likely to see them on the street. *Although,* I thought, *maybe one of my teens will get a chance to talk to them in the safety of the local market.*

The summer went by fast—full of fun and excitement. We swam in the Frio River, the kids worked hard on their prayer notebooks and several went to a retreat at a local campground. One week, I was even privileged to get another nineteen-year-old partner, Rachle Silva, to help lead a Vacation Bible School at the Spanish church across town. Our successful week ended with a rousing parents' night. We stood by proudly as our young charges sang and signed "Jesus Loves Me" in American Sign Language.

Afterward, the stars above the town twinkled in a cloudless sky as Rachle and I waited in the deserted parking lot for the elderly pastor to drive us home.

I noticed two teen boys walking down the road toward the church. As they approached, the street light broke the shadows to reveal their faces. My heart pounded. The faces belonged to Mundo and Manuel, the teen drug runners my youth group had been praying for.

*This could mean trouble,* I realized as I watched the boys advance. I was relieved when they passed us by. But a few minutes later, the boys returned.

I tried to ignore them.

"Hey, Linda!" a drunken voice called out.

Goose bumps crawled up my arms. *Bad sign. They've been drinking, and they know my name—even though we've never been introduced!*

"What do you want?" I called into the darkness.

"Come over here!"

Rachle shouted back, "No, you come over here."

The two young men approached. Even under the dimness of the street light, I could see hate filling their bloodshot eyes. "What do you want?" I called again, trying to sound calm.

Manuel stepped forward, crowding me with his alcoholic breath. I stepped back, trying to escape the fumes.

"What do we want?" Manuel slurred. "We want you to prove that God is real!"

I swallowed hard. "God loves you. His Son died for the things you've done wrong. In fact, John 3:16 says, 'For God so loved the world, that he gave his only begotten Son, that whosoever believeth in him should not perish, but have everlasting life' (KJV).

"If you ask Him, He will forgive you and will be a part of your life."

"I don't want you to tell me about God. I want you to prove to me that He is real," Manuel replied, stepping even closer.

"I can prove it only by telling you He is in my heart."

Manuel towered over me, his voice cold and threatening. "That's not good enough. We want you to prove there is a God, and we want you to prove it *now!*"

As Manuel had encroached into my space, I backed into a wall. Now I could back up no farther. I glanced around nervously. *There's nowhere to run and no one around to help.*

*Lord,* I prayed, *there is nothing more I can say to these young men to prove You are real. Would You please take over now? It's up to You.*

As I finished my silent prayer, the beautiful starry night changed. A strong wind arose; swirling sand pelted our faces. High above our heads a cloud blotted out the stars as it broke the blackness with jagged streaks of lightning.

Everyone froze while the wind whipped our hair and blinded our eyes. Rachle shouted above the booms of thunder, "See, that's God telling you He is real!"

No one argued.

The frightened boys ran one way and Rachle and I ran the other. A few minutes later, the cloud passed and calm returned. When Rachle and I reached the home where we were staying, we were still awed. We sat on our bed in the safety of our little bedroom and smiled at each other.

"You know," I said, repeating myself for the hundredth time, "that really was God. He really was there."

"Yes," Rachle agreed, nodding as if in a trance. "He was awesome!"

The excitement of our discovery gave us a sleepless but joyful night. And I learned that God can reveal Himself—not only to two naive college women but also to two teen smugglers who dared to ask for proof of His existence.

I've also learned to be careful about what I pray for—careful to pray for whatever impossible dream He may put into my heart. After all, I never know what miracles God may perform unless I dare to ask.

From *Faith Never Shrinks in Hot Water,* © 1996 by Linda E. Shepherd. Used by permission.

Linda Evans Shepherd is a nationally known speaker and member of the National Speakers Association. She was named 1997 Colorado Christian Author of the Year. Her latest books include her devotional novel, *Reunion of the Heart,* her book on friendship, *Encouraging Hands, Encouraging Hearts,* and *Share Jesus Without Fear,* the latter written with evangelist Bill Fay. She is a mother of two, has been married twenty years, and resides in Longmont, Colorado.

Web site: http://www. sheppro.com
E-mail: Lswrites@aol. com.

## Learning to Encourage

## *Beverly Hamel*

When my dearest friend and I were fifteen years old, her mom left her father and the family. This left Mary Ellen to be mother to her two younger sisters: cooking, cleaning, making sure they all had clothes to wear for school the next day, checking on their homework—all the while driving herself to make good grades.

I looked up to Mary Ellen, because I was still a wimpy little griper while she, despite a traumatic loss in her life, was doing all those domestic things I hadn't yet learned.

I couldn't imagine how their mom could have left like that. *My* mom felt that raising my brothers and me was a joy, a privilege and a responsibility from the Lord.

One day, my mom arranged for all three of the girls to come over to our house after school. That day, I began to grow up. Sitting on my mom's bed,

187

the girls told mom and me everything they had to do every day. Finally, after they were all talked out, my dear mother began to encourage them to put God first in their lives. Mary Ellen was having trouble with cooking, so mom gave her some tips and some recipes.

After they left, I heard my mother crying in her room. She was crying out of pity toward the girls—because they all had to work too hard for girls their ages.

I felt jealous. I felt that, well, they weren't my sisters, but here was my mom telling them how to do stuff like she usually did for me. I mentioned it to her. She wasn't very happy about my jealousy. With great compassion, she reminded me that I had both my parents and those girls didn't. She said firmly but lovingly that I was the one who would have to adjust, because if talking with those little girls would help them, she was going to help them any way she could.

Mary Ellen knows her Savior now. The Lord, and the encouragement she received from my wonderful mother over the years, helped her find the peace of spirit to finally reconcile with her own mom.

That incident when I was fifteen has been a driving catalyst for me to help children and teenagers come to know and to serve God. Since that time, I have come to know my Savior better and also the Father of all, who also knows how to mother the motherless. He is the "Father of compassion and the God of all comfort, who comforts us in all our troubles, so that we can comfort those in any trouble with the comfort we ourselves have received from God" (2 Corinthians 1:3-4).

While working with children in "Little Cambodia," in San Diego, I have seen a prevalence of children with no one at home to encourage them. Teenage girls of that culture are considered of the lowest rank and are not usually respected. Yet God led me and showed me how to encourage them.

The first child God brought my way taught me a wonderful truth. When I first met her, Saron was only eleven, but already she was feeling the stigma of being only a baby factory. But once she and the others accepted the idea that *God* thought they were wonderful, they drank it in like water. They seemed to blossom like flowers in a garden. They only needed to know that Someone bigger than they were loved them.

I felt like the pied piper; wherever I went in that neighborhood, they seemed to attach themselves to me. It reminded me of the Scripture in Zechariah 8:23 that gives a promise from God that people will latch onto the skirt of a child of God, saying, "Let us go with you, because we have heard that God is with you." It's amazing how the love of God sets people free and releases hope and joy.

A twelve-year-old black boy came to my door one day shortly after I had spoken with him on the street. Abibi's home life was terrible because his

mother was a prostitute for drugs. He was concerned for his sister, who then was three years old.
He didn't want her to know what was happening
after she was put to bed at night. Abibi learned
that God loved him and that he had worth, despite his mother's actions. He heard the gospel of
Jesus Christ and began to grow in God by leaps
and bounds. Right now, he is working his way
through high school. This young man, who had no
reason to laugh and enjoy himself, has many reasons now. He does it quite frequently these days!

Abibi's little sister also came to know the Lord
when he kept bringing her over to my house with
him. The last time I heard from Abibi, his sister
was a "little preacher" to her friends at school.

My mother put in me the idea of being an en-
courager and helper to those in need, and my
heavenly Father has led me to those who needed
it. I've found out that the more I encourage others, the more I receive encouragement when I'm
in need. No, life isn't always fun. But praise the
Lord, He takes us through the storms, encouraging and helping us to bounce back in victory.

> *We who are strong ought to bear with the
> failings of the weak and not to please our-
> selves. Each of us should please his neigh-
> bor for his good, to build him up. (Romans
> 15:1-2)*

Beverly Hamel was born and grew up in Kansas City, Missouri. The navy stationed her at San Diego, California where she later met her husband at Bible college. For eleven years, she taught outdoor Bible studies to children from Southeast Asia. She is now in the process of writing a devotional book for teens.

# Two Teen Stories from France

## Janey L. DeMeo

My work with Anthony and Vanessa in southern France is longstanding, especially with Anthony, whom I've known since he was very little. His mother has been in our church for many years, and he has come to our Christian school since he was small.

I have a deep passion for children—especially hurting children. I pray for them and get myself involved whenever I can. I occasionally teach the youth in the church's youth group and in our school. I also work with them one-on-one from time to time.

To put these two stories in perspective, here are some things you, the reader, might keep in mind: The number one cause of death among young people in France is suicide. Very few hear about God. If you are a Christian you are mocked. Born-again Christians are a small minority—estimated

193

to be only one-half of one percent of the French population. Imagine how few of these are young people!

There is just about no such thing in France as a thirteen-year-old virgin. That would be a joke to most people. My fifteen-year old daughter goes to the doctor, and each time she is asked what type of contraception she uses. When she explains she's a virgin and plans to stay that way until she is married, they look at her as if she's nuts.

It's a hard, dark country. Children are taught through humiliation, not rewards. Thus, they grow up insecure, aggressive and depressed. I understand that more people take antidepressants here than in any other country in the world.

Anthony and Vanessa, along with some of their Christian friends, are lights in this darkness. Both are somewhat quiet and reserved—deep thinkers and quietly determined. Both are great soul winners. Both are "real" teens with "real" struggles, who have found God as the Source of all their hope and joy. Here are their stories:

### Vanessa

Tears were trickling down Vanessa's cheeks and into her breakfast bowl when Steven, her nine-year-old brother, bounced into the kitchen. She quickly grabbed the dish towel—dirty, like the rest of the house—to wipe her eyes. She did not want

Steven to see her crying, adding to the pain he already knew. She knew she had to be strong for him.

Quickly she made his breakfast, scooping aside the leftover wine bottles, and then helped him get ready for the day. The children then crept apprehensively into their mother's room, attempting to say good-bye before leaving for school. But, as usual, their mother was still deep in sleep—cloyed by what she had drunk the night before.

It was just another day in fourteen-year-old Vanessa's miserable life. Each day it was the same: Vanessa's mother, finally aroused from her alcoholic stupor, would wake up possessed by rage and reach for the nearest bottle. Each day, Vanessa would assume the household responsibilities and cover for her little brother. Deprived of living her own life, she was forced to be housekeeper, "mother" and cook—enslaved to a life of hardship.

Vanessa's parents had divorced when she was only nine years old. For as long as she could remember, her mother drank. Sometimes she would drag Vanessa and Steven into smoky bars so she could drink. The children were heartbroken time and time again to see her go off with different men, shattering any illusion they could have of becoming a proper family. Their lives resembled a rubbish heap, filled with broken pieces and bad odors.

Compared to the burdens weighing heavily on her heart, the hefty books Vanessa carried to school every day seemed but featherweight. And even when the Mediterranean sun was shining outside, her room still looked dark to her. Many times she felt she could hardly bear to face another day of this kind of life.

Then, one day, life drastically changed for Vanessa. That was the day she was introduced to real hope. Gaelle, her fifteen-year-old girlfriend who had just become a Christian, described to Vanessa how her newfound faith in Christ had changed her own life.

Vanessa had never heard such inspiring words in her life. Coming from a Catholic background, she already believed in God, but she now realized that she did not know Him personally. She had never read the Bible and knew nothing of the gospel message. That day, she prayed to ask Christ into her heart. She didn't understand much—she didn't know how to explain it all to others—but she knew she had a real Friend now: her beloved Savior.

Vanessa was truly transformed. As she began going regularly to a lively church and to the church youth club, she still couldn't understand the messages, but her soul was soothed by the loving atmosphere and the purity of the worship. Having only attended dead churches before on rare occasions, to her this church with its young people, its lively singing and its warmth was like an oasis in a dry land.

Vanessa's salvation was timely. She says, "If I'd not met God then, I would surely have done something stupid because I just couldn't take any more!"

She can hardly talk of this time without tears welling up in her eyes: "Now I realize God really came to seek me and to draw me to Himself," she says. "When I see my life before—how lonely I was—I realize I had nothing to lean on and no one to talk to. I couldn't even really trust my friends. Now I have Jesus to lean on and lots of new friends."

As Vanessa has grown in Christ, she has come to understand and appreciate the teaching of the Word of God. She says, "I've always loved the singing because it shows me God's love, but at first I couldn't understand the sermons. Then later I could, and they always met my precise situations."

Since Vanessa's conversion, she has shared the gospel on many occasions. Her father and her brother Steven have given their hearts to Christ. During a Teen Surf Camp on the Atlantic Coast, Vanessa—then sixteen—led two girls her age to Christ.

Because of her faith, she is often cast aside at school, mocked and rejected. But compared to the pain she used to feel before walking with God, she wouldn't change this for anything. She also understands the immense privilege of knowing God in a country where atheism and alcoholism rule. She knows that the rejection is normal because her life is a light in the darkness. She is encouraged because she has found a beautiful family in the body of Christ where she is loved and accepted.

After finishing school, Vanessa would like to be a social worker, specifically working with teenage delinquents. "People become delinquents because they lack being loved, but true love only comes from God," she states. "I want to show them there's Someone who really loves them, that there is real hope."

And real hope is certainly what Vanessa's godly countenance and bubbling laughter inspire.

### Anthony

It was a drizzly day in southern France. Not a typical day for that time of year, but one that clearly matched fourteen-year-old Anthony's mood. He was sick at home, brooding with the flu and feeling rotten.

Since giving his heart to Christ at a very young age, blond-haired, green-eyed Anthony knew God was at work in his life. He had delivered him from much of the pain he had endured since his father left home when Anthony was born, leaving his mother destitute and with the sole burden of rearing baby Anthony and two-year old Estelle.

Early in his life, their home was one of tears, anger and anxiety. And although Anthony was too young to remember the details, he absorbed the anguish. He occasionally saw his father (now living with another woman) but felt abandoned, cast aside and confused. Then, when his mother gave her heart to Christ, their story began to change.

Anthony's father lived a worldly life, void of God's presence, but his mother and older sister had chosen to follow God. Anthony had too! He gave his heart to Christ at five years of age. But following God was not always easy—particularly when Anthony became a teenager.

At times, Anthony would feel the weight of his mother's worries—finances, loneliness, not having a car and so on. But a major burden was his gnawing awareness that he lacked a father in his life. Not that he lacked paternal affection as such; he was well taken care of by loving men of God in his church. Different pastors invested in Anthony. He was loved—even when he went through difficult times or, on some occasions, revolt!

There were nonetheless times when the struggle would surface. "I remember being only seven when my dad came to get me for a visit," he explains. "He hadn't called for a long time, so I was surprised and upset. I told him about Christ, and that I didn't want to be influenced by his worldly lifestyle. I repeated this same thing another time he came and now he has not come back to see me since.

"At eleven years of age, I knew that I was saved, but I wondered, considering my struggle with not having a father, where God was in my life. Thanks to my mother, the teen club pastors and church, I finally concluded that God wanted my life this way and that He would still bless me somehow. I went through periods of doubt, but the more I grew, the less it was a problem."

Anthony was fortunate to go at a young age to a Christian school—one of only a handful in France—and this helped him tremendously. He began going to church when he was ten.

"At first," he remembers, "I found it boring, and didn't understand; so I thought it wasn't for me. By the time I was eleven, I was asked to work with the sound system, which I love. I began understanding the messages and applying them. This really strengthened me. The teen club helped a lot too because the messages were specially adapted for youth."

On that drizzly day when Anthony was at home with the flu, he had no idea a miracle was ready to embrace him and build up his faith. He had assisted at an international conference the previous fall, and he had loved hearing the different preachers and meeting people from all over the world. Now he had heard there would be another international conference in Budapest. He badly wanted to go and began praying for a way. It seemed financially impossible—and he didn't even have a passport. But he kept thinking of the thousands of people going.

"Then someone called and told me that the money for the conference was paid," he says. "At that time I had the flu and wasn't well at all. And I still had no passport. Usually it takes three weeks to process a passport but I got mine within one week! It came just the day before I was scheduled to leave.

"I'd always heard of people who got gifts at the last minute, but I never thought I would be one! I saw the hand of God and I saw He wanted me at this conference. I saw God's hand on my life as a loving Father. The conference blessed me and made me grow. Now I know I'd never leave the church. I'm seeking God to see what I should do in the future. I'd like to be a pastor."

Anthony sees his responsibility to pray for and work with other hurting children—especially those in the street, without parents or money. "I try to identify and to understand their problems," he says. His compassion is genuine.

It will be interesting to see where God sends this young man as He raises him up to be a pastor.

Janey DeMeo is the wife of Pastor Louis DeMeo, missionary and founder of their local church, a Christian day school and *L'Institut Theologique*, a Bible college in Uchaud, France. Her diverse roles include mothering their two children, writing and teaching women at the Bible institute—many of whom now serve on other foreign fields such as Africa, Romania, Hungary, England, Ireland and Switzerland.

Janey, who is British, has authored *Mon Dieu, Ces Enfants!* a parenting book published in France, and her articles have appeared in many American and French Christian magazines. Her passion for suffering children is reflected in all she does. She is the founder of two corporations: *Sauver les Enfants* in France and Orphans First in the United States. She and her family travel often to different countries working with hurting children and spreading the gospel.

Web site: www.ggwo.org/orphansfirst
E-mail: LDeMeo@compuserve.com

# The Day I First Got Hooked

## Jeff Crume

It was a rainy day in Houston, Texas. I stood there, heart racing and palms sweating. Then I heard the words, "Please help me welcome Jeff Crume."

I was at the Harris County Children's Protective Services facility, and this was my first speech. My audience? About thirty-five young people, ages twelve to sixteen—kids who had been abandoned, abused, neglected and rejected, some by their parents, others by society.

Applause rose from my small audience. I glanced out over (what seemed to me) a sea of faces—young people eagerly waiting to hear a message that would let them know that they mattered, that they were special, that they too could dare to dream and could even make their dreams come true.

In my heart, I felt the love of Jesus as I spoke to them, and yet it seemed to me that I stuttered, stammered and stepped on my tongue throughout most of the presentation.

"What do you want to be when you grow up?" I asked the group.

A young teen in the front row spoke up eagerly, "I want to be a doctor!" A pretty girl on my left spoke in melodious tones, "I'm going to be a model." And yet another voice from the back of the room blurted out, "I want to be a speaker like you."

I thought, *WOW! That's cool!* No one had ever wanted to be like *me* before!

Then suddenly, as if there weren't another soul in the room, my attention was drawn to a little girl in the second row to my right. Her knees were tucked tightly up under her, and her head was bent low, almost in her lap.

I walked over, knelt down beside her and asked, "What would *you* like to be when you grow up, sweetheart?"

Slowly she raised her head, tears streaming down her cheeks, and whispered, "I don't know, I don't know, *I don't know!*"

Abandoned at birth, she was now twelve years old and had been in twelve different foster homes. I knelt there, my heart racing, my palms sweating, tears welling up in my eyes. This was it—I knew I had to say something to help her.

I softly whispered the only words I could find: "Sweetheart, you can have any dream you want. Look for your own dream and hold on to it. The one thing no one can ever take away from you is your dream."

I smiled into her sad brown eyes and suddenly saw a flicker of hope. That's when I *knew* I was hooked! That moment in Houston changed my life forever. Giving hope to hopeless kids became my passion.

The greatest tragedy in the world is a child without a dream. Though this story speaks of only one, it represents millions of other young people who live each day without knowing who they are or how they fit into this picture called life.

And the little sad-eyed girl? Well, I went back to say good-bye the day of my flight home. The directors at the facility said the change in that child was nothing short of a miracle. She had asked for crayons and started coloring pictures of her dreams. The pictures were taped up all over the walls of her tiny room. I didn't get to see her that day, but she had heard I was coming and left me the following message:

*Dear Mr. Crume, thank you for helping me believe in myself. I'm holding on to my dreams and I'm not letting go!*

I guess that moment changed *her* life as well as mine.

That little girl is really the reason I am still out there speaking today. I share her story all over the country. That day in Houston she needed to hear that she could have dreams and that no one could ever take them from her. That day she felt the love of Jesus through me. That love is in me and I earnestly wanted to pass it along to her.

I believe that as Christians we have a responsibility to be examples and messengers of Christ to those around us. I thank God that I had the opportunity to tell that little girl how special she was, how valuable she was to this world. Was that a message from Christ? I believe it was!

Years later, I am still hooked on helping others hold onto their dreams, discover their true potential and pursue their lives with purpose and passion. Getting hooked this way was the best thing that has ever happened to me. I invite *you* to do the same.

Speaker, trainer and author Jeff Crume delivers a straight-from-the-heart message to teens, teachers, parents and professional groups. He challenges and inspires listeners to hold on to their dreams, discover their true potential and pursue life with purpose and passion. In October, 1999, Jeff and his wife, Jodi, launched a new full-time national ministry called Armed & Dangerous Ministries—"Standing in the Gap," aimed at helping teens cope with the reality or threat of violence inflicted on them in schools and churches. Jeff, Jodi and their daughter, Kami, live in Southern California.

Address: P.O. Box 2496, Orange, CA 92859
E-mail: JeffC261@aol.com

## Advice from the Experts

*Get wisdom, get understanding. . . .*
*Do not forsake wisdom, and she will*
*protect you.*

(Proverbs 4:5-6)

As you scan the titles in this last section, you may think some of these stories and comments are written more for your parents than for you as a teen. But wait! This is your chance to "listen in" and perhaps gain a better understanding of where your parents are coming from and why they act the way they do. This information and these stories will also give you a head start on being a great parent yourself someday.

The contributors in this section have spent a lifetime in the study of human behavior. They have a deep understanding of psychology and a profound love of God—and teens.

Others whose stories appear throughout this book could certainly be included in this section as well. These experts, by the nature of their work and the "fruit" of their lives, have demonstrated a Christlike love for people—especially for teenagers. The advice they offer can be a great tool to help teens and their parents find a starting point for some long-overdue discussions. Who knows—maybe these discussions will mend a damaged relationship, build a new relationship or at least open a door to better understanding. That is my hope and prayer.

# Being a Dad in Tough Times

## Josh McDowell

As a child, I never knew a father's love. I never benefited from a father's example. I can't remember a single time when my father took me somewhere alone and spent time with me. I can't remember feeling proud of my father or imitating him. In fact, I hated him.

I grew up on a 150-acre dairy farm just outside a small town in Michigan. Everyone knew everyone else in that town and, of course, everyone knew about my father and his drinking. My teenage buddies made jokes about him, and I laughed too, hoping my laughter would hide my pain.

I hated him for the shame he caused me, but also for the way he treated my mother. Sometimes I'd go out to the barn and find my mother lying in the manure behind the cows, beaten so badly she couldn't get up. Sometimes when he came home in a drunken stupor, I would drag him out to the barn, tie him to a stall and leave him there to "sleep it off." As a teenager, I would tie his feet with a noose that ended around his neck, hoping he would choke himself while trying to get free. When my mother died the month of my high school graduation, I blamed my father.

Though God generously brought about a reconciliation with my father after I became a Christian, and even allowed me to help him trust Christ for salvation (fourteen months before he died of a heart attack), I became a father with an acute sense of how unprepared I was to be a father.

You may not have had such a poor relationship with your father, but you may share some of my realization that parenthood may be the scariest job in the world. To make matters worse, there's nowhere to obtain a license for fatherhood. There are very few job requirements. And most of us must learn on the job, by trial and error—mostly by error! In fact, someone has observed that most people don't really become good at being a parent until their children have become parents!

Over the past several years, I have observed and counseled scores of fellow strugglers—well-meaning dads who feel overwhelmed by the job of becoming an effective father. Many admit that they're fumbling in the juggling act of marriage, career and fatherhood. Most feel trapped by their intense work schedules and the accompanying pressures. Many feel limited by a lack of practical fathering skills, by a difficult marriage or by unhealthy patterns in their own lives.

Moreover, the challenges of fatherhood are even more pronounced today than ever before.

We—and our children—live in a world that often threatens our marriages, our families and our children. We live in a culture that rejects the truth of the Bible, that mocks biblical morality, glorifies sex and violence and laughs at drunkenness and rudeness. We live in a society that has largely rejected the notions of truth and morality, a society that has somehow lost the ability to decide what is true and what is right, a society in which truth has become a matter of taste and morality has been replaced by individual preference.

We are faced with the daunting task of raising children amidst a culture in crisis. It is little wonder that many men face the task of fathering with fear and trembling. But fathering is not only, in many respects, the most frightening job in the world, it is also among the most critically needed jobs in the world.

The task of being a father is of critical importance, and it has never been more so than in this day and age. A child's relationship with Dad is a decisive factor in that young man or woman's health, development and happiness. Consider the following, well-documented findings:

- Dr. Loren Moshen, of the National Institute of Mental Health, analyzed U.S. census figures and found the absence of a father to be a stronger factor than poverty in contributing to juvenile delinquency.

- A group of Yale behavioral scientists studied delinquency in forty-eight cultures around the world and found that crime rates were highest among adults who as children had been raised solely by women.

- A study of thirty-nine teenage girls who were suffering from the anorexia nervosa eating disorder showed that thirty-six of them had one common denominator: the lack of a close relationship with their fathers.

Based on my interaction with hundreds of moms, dads and kids, I would agree with those findings. Not only that, but the results of those studies correspond closely with recent research among youth in evangelical Christian churches as well.

Not long ago, I commissioned a survey of more than 3,700 teens in evangelical churches—the most extensive survey of evangelical youth ever conducted. The research, assembled by The Barna Research Group, underscored the importance of the father connection with a child.

Of the 3,795 youth surveyed in that study, eighty-two percent attended an evangelical church weekly and eighty-six percent said they had made a commitment to trust Christ as their Savior and Lord. Yet the study showed that fifty-four percent of teens and pre-teens in evangelical church families say they seldom or never talk with their father about their personal concerns (compared to twenty-six percent who say they seldom or never talk with Mom about such things). One in every four young people surveyed stated that they *never* have a meaningful conversation with their father. More than two in five (forty-two percent) say they seldom or never do something special with their father that involves "just the two of you." And one in five say their father seldom or never shows his love for them.[1]

At the same time, the study reveals that youth who are "very close" to their parents are:

- more likely to feel "very satisfied" with their life
- more likely to abstain from sexual intercourse
- more likely to espouse biblical standards of truth and morality
- more likely to attend church
- more likely to read their Bible consistently
- more likely to pray daily

The research—not only among Christian youth, but among all young people—strongly indicates that the father connection is a crucial factor in a child's health, development and happiness. This does not mean that mothers are not important; however, it does underscore the fact that, in most cases Mom has been there, doing her job, taking care of the children, talking to the children and spending time with the children. As a result, it seems children have come to expect Mom to be accessible, loving, communicative and accepting.

With Dad, however, the law of supply and demand comes into play. In many cases he is less accessible, less involved or less communicative. With attention and time from him in short supply, an aura of greater significance builds around that relationship. Just like all of us, our kids crave what they do not have, and in too many cases they do not have a close relationship with their dads.

That is why the father connection is the most important factor in the life of your children, regardless of their ages. Dad, your relationship with your sons and daughters now is a verifiably critical factor in their growth in wisdom, stature and favor with God and man. You can make all the difference in your child's self-esteem, regard for others and sense of purpose.

True, there are moments when some of us wonder if our children are really a reward from the Lord! But when you think that Almighty God has entrusted to us the task of preparing young lives for responsible, worthwhile adulthood, the mission takes on eternal significance. Fathering is indeed a privilege given by the Lord—a matchless opportunity to pour our lives into those we love so dearly.

I invite you to make the commitment with me that, no matter how tough it may get, no matter how unresponsive our kids may be, no matter which way the road may bend in the future—we dedicate ourselves to the privilege and responsibility of conscientious, loving, involved, communicative fathering.

I read a book called *The One Minute Manager,* in which the authors encourage managers to move around among their employees in an effort to "catch them doing something right," so they can offer appreciation and encouragement for their employees' efforts.

That phrase turned things around for me, and I adopted a new "father motto." It was "try to catch your kids doing something right." When I saw Sean taking out the trash, I would say, "Sean, thanks for remembering to take the trash out." When I caught Kelly doing homework, I would say, "Honey, I appreciate the way you study." When I entered a room to find Katie picking up her toys, I'd say, "Katie, I really appreciate how you take care of your toys." This technique of trying to catch my kids doing something right mightily influenced my attitude toward my kids, and I think it reinforced positive behavior in them.

The child whose father provides godly discipline—discipline that is loving, clear, consistent—is likely to reap a harvest of respect, peace and righteousness. He equips his children to learn self-discipline, a quality that will help them lead lives that are healthy—emotionally, socially, spiritually and physically. He helps his children avoid the often tragic consequences of unwise behavior.

He enables his children to enjoy the blessing of a good reputation. He promotes harmony in his children's minds and hearts and in their relationships with others.

That's what God's discipline accomplishes in me, and that's what I wish for my children. I want to be the kind of father who by his comfort and support equips his children to stand up to unhealthy peer pressure, battle insecurity, build healthy friendships and earn the respect and admiration of their peers. I want to be the kind of father my Father is.

1 Josh McDowell and Bob Hostetler, *Right from Wrong* (Dallas, TX: Word Publishing, 1994), 255.

From *The Father Connection* by Josh McDowell. © 1996 Josh McDowell. All rights reserved. Lifeway Christian Resources, Nashville, TN. Used by permission.

Josh McDowell is author and co-author of more than fifty-two books on teens and family relationships. After graduating from Wheaton College and Talbot Theological Seminary, he joined the staff of Campus Crusade for Christ, and has remained a representative for that organization throughout his lifetime. Josh is one of the world's most popular youth speakers, having spoken to more than 7 million young people in eighty-four countries, including 700 university and college campuses. He and his wife, Dottie, and their family live in the Dallas area where he heads the Josh McDowell Ministry.

# When the Odds Are Great

## Ken Davis

There are very few model families. All families struggle and have problems. Many teenagers come from single-parent families. Many families face illness, financial struggles, alcoholism, drug dependency and other major problems. If the love of Christ is only effective in perfect homes, then His love means nothing, because there are no perfect homes.

You are not alone. Right this minute, there are thousands of kids facing the problems that you thought were unique to you. I want to encourage you to believe that the power and love of Jesus Christ has transformed lives in the most horrible of circumstances, from concentration camps to war zones. No matter what your situation, He can do the same for you.

There is no guarantee that your problems will go away, but God promises that you don't have to face those problems alone. With the power of

His love you can find peace and have a profound impact on the people you live with. My files are full of testimonies from moms and dads who got their lives straightened out because they saw God's love in the lives of their children.

God sent Jesus Christ for sinners—for imperfect people in imperfect families. He healed the sick and ministered to the poor. The instructions written in the Word of God are for you—not for some hypothetical perfect family. The blessings that await those who follow Christ are also for you. There is no problem so big that He can't meet your need.

## What If My Parents Aren't Christians?

If your parents have never trusted Christ for the forgiveness of their sins, you're faced with a double dilemma. First, you want them to understand your beliefs; second, you want them to experience the same forgiveness and joy you have. On both counts, the key is clear communication of your faith and a disciplined life that demonstrates that faith.

I know many Christian teenagers who live fairly clean lives but don't demonstrate their faith at home. They would never consider taking a drink or smoking a joint because of what it would do to their testimony. But they treat their families like the lowest forms of life on earth. The greatest witness you will have to your parents is the way you live at home. Your willingness to forgive, your desire to be obedient and your efforts to love your family will carry more weight than all the preaching in the world.

Although it may seem that they expect you to be perfect, they don't. They know you aren't perfect because they live with you. But they will be watching to see how Christianity works for imperfect people. Why? Because they know that they are imperfect, and if it works for you they may conclude that it will also work for them.

## When Your Parents Are Wrong

It's always difficult to be right when the people who have authority over you are wrong. A parent's authority makes it much easier for him to say, "You're wrong!" But what if your parents are wrong? Do you ignore the problem because you have no power to change it? Or do you risk the problems that can come with confronting someone who is in authority over you? Confrontation—especially that kind—isn't easy, and the risks of being misunderstood are high. Here are some suggestions:

1. Be careful about making any judgments. It's easy to misjudge your parents and falsely accuse them of being wrong. More than one teenager who has made that accusation has, after carefully reconsidering the situation and letting some time go by, realized that his parents had been right all along. Weigh the evidence well before you jump to conclusions.

2. Give them the right to be wrong. Teenagers often expect perfection from their parents. Your parents are no different from you. They struggle to do right and sometimes fall flat on their faces. Parents are tempted; they sin; they even make stupid mistakes.

   Give them a break. If your mother and father struggle with sin, then love and forgive them. That attitude will allow you to approach them with understanding love when you confront them.

3. Don't try to confront in the midst of emotion. Wait until both you and your parents have cool heads before you try to express your concerns. If you confront them during emotional peaks, any of you might say things that should never be spoken. Wait until you're calm.

4. Avoid accusation. You'll get much further if you talk about how their behavior makes you feel, rather than blatantly accusing your parents of being wrong.

A boy from Denver lived with the worsening alcoholism of his father for years before he finally talked with him about it. On the way to a basketball game, he told his dad how deeply it hurt to see him ruining his life. His father bluntly responded that it was none of the boy's business what he did with his life.

For many teenagers that would have been the end of the conversation. This boy, with wisdom beyond his years, replied, "Dad, I love you. That makes it my business."

I would love to report that the conversation was the turning point in this father's life and that he never touched a drop of booze again. That's not the case. But that father and son never made it to the basketball game—they spent that evening in a truck stop, opening up to each other as they had not done for years. Now, the father no longer struggles alone, and the son understands his father more than ever before. If the son had responded to his father's first rude reply with accusations, the communication would have ended on the spot.

During a visit to my parents' home I was confronted by my ten-year-old daughter. The problem was that, when visiting my parents, I often would allow my language to become vulgar and crude, maybe in an attempt to express my adulthood to parents who had been very strict when I was young. Regardless of the reason, the language was inappropriate and didn't go unnoticed by Traci.

While she was preparing for bed one evening, she began to cry. It took me a long time to get her to talk about what was causing her sadness. When she finally did speak, her words cut to my very soul.

She didn't imply that I was a terrible person or accuse me of having a dirty mouth. Instead, she told me how my talk confused and hurt her. I tried to justify my actions with several good excuses, but the more I talked the more I realized that she was right and I was so wrong. I made a promise to be more careful with my tongue, and I asked her to help me.

I can honestly say that her confrontation that night has changed the way I talk. She made me aware that many people were watching my life, expecting to see consistency in my behavior. Her confrontation wasn't an insult. It was the expression of a girl who respected her father and was disappointed by his behavior. She wanted me to be a first-class dad wherever I was. She was right, and that's just what I want to be.

## When There Is a Crisis in the Family

Crisis puts an extra load of stress on a family that can draw them closer together or blow them apart. Divorce, illness, death and a host of other devastating events can test the bonds that hold a family together. Each time your family goes through a crisis the psychological complexity of that experience could fill a book—and, in each of those books, your ability to cope would always come back to your attitude.

Are you willing to consider the needs of the other members of the family above your own? Are you willing to pitch in and provide some of the teamwork needed to bring a family through rough times? Families that draw closer during a crisis do so because the crisis helps them realize how much they need each other.

Does it sound as if I'm suggesting that, if we just pray and be good, everything will be better? It doesn't always work that way—sometimes help must come from outside the family. If the problems you're facing seem overwhelming, it's important that you seek help from a competent Christian counselor. Your pastor or youth pastor can be an excellent source of help during difficult times. If they feel unable to help you, they can refer you to someone who can.

When there is physical or sexual abuse, it is absolutely necessary that you get outside help immediately. And if you don't get help from the first person you talk with, keep trying until you do. Many abused children are afraid to tell anyone about how they're being treated because of the terrible problems that will result when people find out. As good counselors will tell you, it will be very difficult at first—but the long-term effects of continued abuse far outweigh the initial pain of telling someone. Don't give up until you get help.

Don't wait for a crisis before calling on the Lord. Instead, start now to build a faith in God that you can draw on when times are rough. If you find yourself facing a crisis now without that reservoir of faith, don't despair. Your simple faith in God to face the moments of helplessness will be met with the strength to take it one step at a time.

No problem is too big for you and the Lord. Philippians 4:13 says: "I can do everything through him who gives me strength." You're no different from David, Abraham, Paul or any of the other Bible heroes who faced difficult odds. With Christ, you can be victorious.

From *How to Live with Your Parents Without Losing Your Mind* by Ken Davis. ©1988 Ken Davis, Zondervan Publishing House, Grand Rapids, MI. Used by permission.

Ken Davis is a best-selling author, frequent radio and television guest and popular motivational speaker who mixes humor with inspiration to delight and enrich audiences of all ages. He has wide experience in working with youth. His books have received national critical acclaim, including the "Book of the Year" award and the Gold Medallion Award. As president of Dynamic Communications International, he teaches speaking skills to ministry professionals and corporate executives. Ken is a graduate of Oak Hills Bible Institute. He and his wife, Diane, live in Colorado and have two daughters.

# Reaching Out to God's Children

## Marian Wright Edelman

Jeannie is in her forties now, but when she was thirteen, tragedy struck her in the form of a drive-by shooting. Someone fired a shotgun blast into the house where she and her family lived. Jeannie was wounded in the eye. Because she had no health insurance, she was turned away by hospital after hospital. By the time her parents found a hospital that would accept her, it was too late. Jeannie lost her eye.

I was practicing law at the time and was absolutely outraged by the absence of access to health care for this child. Jeannie and I became good friends, and I was eventually able to help her get a prosthetic eye. She went on to finish school, have a family and become employed by the Department of Human Services. Whatever help I had been to her was an investment in the

future, an investment that resulted in a wonderful mother and productive citizen.

## Going Back Home

And there were those who made an investment in me and in the whole community of children in my neighborhood. When I went back
home one Thanksgiving, I revisited the house
where I was born, the home in which my parents
raised us children and cared for nieces and
nephews and children from the community who
needed love and care.

In that very house, I and others had created a
project called Freedom School, which is now offered by the Children's Defense Fund. At the
school, children receive academic and cultural
tutoring. This house that is so alive with activity
is a tribute to my parents and the community.
Twenty-seven other schools around the country
have sprung up from this project.

## Role Models

The Freedom School stands so sturdy, right
next to the church my father and mother built. My
parents were incredible role models of faith and
service, of sharing what they had to help others.
They believed in living their faith every day, and
they cared deeply about children—about all people. There were always foster children in our
home. Christmas in our family was about helping
others, delivering coal, food and clothing to those

in need. My father told us, "If you respond to the need around you and trust God, you will never go wrong."

My mother raised twelve foster children after she raised her own five children. The community of my childhood reached out and considered all children its own. When children did not have a place to go, others took them in, and it was this community kinship that enriched all our lives.

Parents are the most important people in children's lives, and as parents, we need to be examples for our children—for all children. More often than not, children do what we *do*, not what we *tell* them to do.

It is so much harder today for parents to keep control of their lives, but this is all the more reason for parents and other adults to make clear that there are certain unchanging values like honesty and service and love that transcend all cultures.

Children need to believe in something, and they are taught what to believe in by the adults around them. They watch us in all of our roles—as parents, citizens, teachers, preachers and politicians—to see how we live. And we can be honest about the struggles and let them see that we may at times make mistakes and fall short of our goals. We are ordinary people who, by the grace of God, can be extraordinary. When hard times come and the wind shears of life hit us, we keep the faith and keep doing the best we can.

## Keeping the Faith

I am able to keep the faith through prayer. I could not live without prayer. I try to find in every minute of every day a recognition of God's presence and also to reflect the presence of God in me through the way I live my life. No, I could not live without prayer.

I remember the words of Jesus: "Ask and it will be given to you; seek and you will find; knock and the door will be opened to you" (Matthew 7:7). Prayer is a way of asking, searching for and finding God. And a life of prayer is a way we can all reach out with love and care to God's children.

Excerpted and abridged from one of Mrs. Edelman's previous "Child Watch" columns. © Children's Defense Fund, 1998. Used with permission. All rights reserved.

*Photo used courtesy of the Children's Defense Fund. Copyright Johnson Publishing. All rights reserved.*

Marian Wright Edelman is founder and president of the Children's Defense Fund, an organization founded in 1973 to educate people about the needs of children. Mrs. Edelman is a graduate of Spelman College and Yale Law School. She has served as director of the Center of Law and Education at Harvard University. A successful author, she has received many honorary degrees and awards including the Albert Schweitzer Humanitarian Prize.

# Fighting Feelings of Inferiority

## James C. Dobson, Ph.D.

What a shame that most teenagers decide they are without much human worth when they're between thirteen and fifteen years of age! It may have happened to some of you even earlier, but in most cases the problem is at its worst during the junior high years.

We *all* have human worth, yet so many young people conclude that they're somehow different—that they're truly inferior—that they lack the necessary ingredients for dignity and worth.

Some of you know that I often work with young people who have these kinds of problems. At one time I served on a high school campus, and there I worked with many teenagers who were struggling with some of the feelings that I've been describing to you.

One day I was walking across the grounds of the high school after the bell had rung. Most of the students were already back in class, but I saw a boy coming toward me in the main hall. I knew that his name was Ronny and that he was in his third year of high school. However, I didn't know him very well. Ronny was one of those many students who remain back in the crowd, never calling attention to themselves and never making friends with those around them. It's easy to forget they're alive because they never allow anybody to get acquainted with them.

When Ronny was about fifteen feet away from me, I saw that he was very upset about something. It was obvious that he was distressed because his face revealed his inner turmoil. As he came a few feet closer, he saw that I was watching him intently. Our eyes locked for a moment, then he looked at the floor as he came closer.

When Ronny and I were parallel, he suddenly covered his face with both hands and turned toward the wall. His neck and ears turned red, and he began to sob and weep. He was not just crying—he seemed to explode with emotion. I put my arm around him and said, "Can I help you, Ronny? Do you feel like talking to me?"

He nodded affirmatively, and I practically had to lead him into my office.

I offered Ronny a chair and closed the door, and I gave him a few minutes to get control of himself before asking him to speak. Then he began to talk to me.

He said, "I've been going to school in this district for eight years, but in all that time I've never managed to make one single friend! Not one. There's not a soul in this high school who cares whether I live or die. I walk to school by myself and I walk home alone. I don't go to football games; I don't go to basketball games or any school activities because I'm embarrassed to sit there all by myself. I stand alone at snack time in the morning, and I eat lunch out in a quiet corner of the campus. Then I go back to class by myself. I don't get along with my dad, and my mother doesn't understand me, and I fight with my sister. And I have nobody! My phone never rings. I have no one to talk to. Nobody knows what I feel and nobody cares. Sometimes I think I just can't stand it anymore!"

I can't tell you how many students have expressed these same feelings to me. One eighth-grade girl named Charlotte felt so bad about herself and about being unpopular that she didn't want to live anymore. She came to school one day and told me she had taken all the pills that were available in the medicine cabinet in an attempt to do away with herself. But she didn't really want to die, or else she wouldn't have told me what she had done. She was actually calling for help. The school nurse and I got her to the hospital just in time to save her life.

Both Charlotte and Ronny are among many thousands of students who are overwhelmed by their own worthlessness, and sometimes this even takes away their desire to live.

Some young people feel inferior and foolish only occasionally, such as when they fail at something very important. But others feel worthless *all* the time. Maybe you're one of those individuals who hurts every day. Have you ever had that big lump in your throat that comes when you feel that nobody cares—that nobody likes you—that maybe they even hate you? Have you ever wished that you could crawl out of your skin and get into another person's body? Do you ever feel like a complete dummy when you're in a group? Would you ever like to descend into a hole and disappear?

Now let's ask some very important questions. Why do so many teenagers feel inferior? Why can't young people grow up liking themselves? Why is it common for people to examine themselves and be bitterly disappointed with the person God has made them? Why is it necessary for everyone to bump his head on the same old rock? These are very good questions, and I believe there are good answers to them.

As young people grow up in our society today, there are three things that teenagers feel they *must* have in order to feel good about themselves. The first of these, and by far the most important, is physical attractiveness. Did you know that about eighty percent of the teenagers

in our society don't like the way they look?
*Eighty percent!*

If you asked ten teenagers what they are most
unhappy about, eight of them would be dissatis-
fied with some feature of their bodies. They feel
ugly and unattractive, and they think about that
problem most of the time.

The second characteristic that young people
don't like about themselves is that they feel unin-
telligent (or dumb). This feeling often begins during the very early school years, when they have
trouble learning in school. Either they have a hard
time learning to read, and they start worrying
about this problem, or else they blurt out answers
that cause everyone to laugh. They gradually start
to  believe that everybody in the classroom (including the teacher) thinks they're stupid, and this
brings the same old feelings of inferiority.

The third value that young people use to mea-
sure their worth is money. You see, they think
the wealthy family is more important than the
poor one, and to be accepted and popular they
have to dress a certain way, or their family has to
have a particular kind of car, or they have to live
in a big house in the right part of town or their
father has to have a certain kind of job. The
young person who can't afford these things
sometimes feels inferior and inadequate.

Beauty, intelligence and money are the three
attributes valued most highly in our society. And
when junior high students first discover that
they are lacking in one (or all three) of these

characteristics, they begin sliding downward in despair. For them, the "bridge" has collapsed and a dark canyon looms below.

Let me offer an encouraging message about the adolescent years, which can be summarized in three words: *normality will return.* By that I mean that you're about to go into a hectic, topsy-turvy world that will make new demands and will confront you with many new challenges. When these stressful moments arrive . . . when you ask a girl for a date and she turns you down, when you don't get invited to the party being given for the popular people, when your parents seem to hassle you over everything you do, when pimples and blackheads attack your forehead like an army of insects, when you wonder if God is really there and if He genuinely cares . . . in those moments when you're tempted to give up, please remember my words: "normality will return."

Just as I was able to predict many of the adolescent experiences that came your way, I can also predict with certainty that this stressful time of life will pass. In some ways, adolescence is like a tunnel that has a known beginning and end. As long as you stay on the road and keep your car moving forward, you can expect to emerge at the other end. Likewise, the anxieties and struggles you have experienced will soon disappear, and a new set of adult pressures will take their place. That's life, as they say.

The final (but most important) advice I can give you is to remain friends with Jesus Christ during the years ahead. He loves you and understands all of your needs and desires. He will be there to share your brightest days and your darkest nights. When you face the important issues of life (choosing a mate, selecting an occupation, etc.), He will guide your footsteps. He gave us that assurance in Proverbs 3:6, which says, "In all thy ways acknowledge him, and he shall direct thy paths" (KJV).

What a comforting promise!

From *Preparing for Adolescence* by Dr. James Dobson, © 1989, Regal Books, Ventura, CA 93003. Used with permission.

James C. Dobson, Ph.D., is founder and president of Focus on the Family, a non-profit organization that produces his internationally syndicated radio programs, heard on more than 3,000 radio facilities in North America and in nine languages in ninety- three other countries. He is the author of numerous best-selling books and has produced several film series, including a seven-part series entitled "Life on the Edge," which is designed to help late teens bridge the gap between adolescence and young adulthood.

Other books in the *Bounce Back* series
Edited and Compiled by Diana L. James
Published by Horizon Books

*Bounce Back* - 1997
*Bounce Back Too* - 1998